M000114328

AN INTIMATE PORTRAIT

EVELYN HART

AN INTIMATE PORTRAIT

EVELYN HART

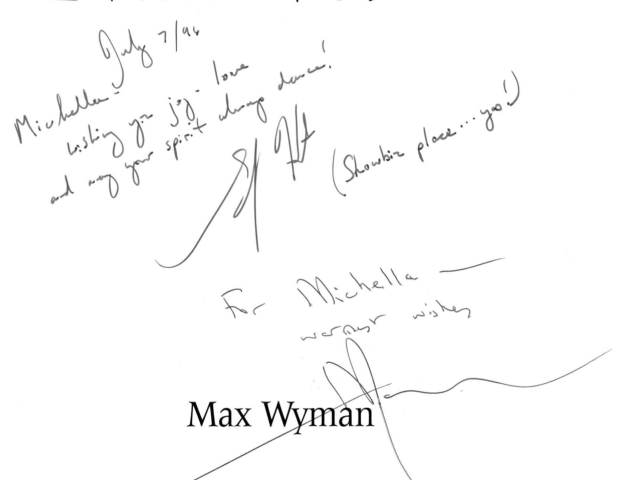

Michella — July 7/96
wishing you joy & love
and may your spirit always dance!
[signature]
(Showbiz place... yes!)

For Michella —
warmest wishes
[signature]

Max Wyman

M&S

Copyright © 1991 Max Wyman

All rights reserved. The use of any part of this publication,
transmitted in any form or by any means, electronic,
mechanical, photocopying, recording, or otherwise, or
stored in a retrieval system, without the prior consent of
the publisher – or, in the case of photocopying or other
reprographic copying, a licence from Canadian
Reprography Collective – is an infringement of
the copyright law.

Canadian Cataloguing in Publication Data
Wyman, Max, 1939–
Evelyn Hart, an intimate biography

Includes index.
ISBN 0–7710–9038–2

1. Hart, Evelyn, 1956–   .   2. Ballerinas – Canada
– Biography.   I. Title.

GV1785.H3W8 1991   792.8'092   C91–094449–0

Printed and bound in Canada.
The paper used in this book is acid-free.

McClelland & Stewart Inc.
The Canadian Publishers
481 University Avenue
Toronto, Ontario
M5G 2E9

For Susan.

And for Henny,
in memoriam

CONTENTS

AN INTIMATE PORTRAIT

EVELYN HART

PREFACE

Critics rarely have the gift of prophecy, regardless of what they might think in their more deluded moments. But sometimes they hit on things despite themselves. The first time I noticed Evelyn Hart's dancing was in November 1977. She was in her second season with the Royal Winnipeg Ballet as a member of the corps de ballet. Promotion to soloist rank was a season ahead; her first, gold-medal successes in international competition were almost three years away.

The company was in Vancouver for a week of *Nutcracker* performances, and this skinny, nervous girl had been chosen to dance the role of Louise, the big sister to the ballerina-child who has all the adventures in John Neumeier's radical reworking of the classic Christmas entertainment. David Moroni, a former company principal dancer who had become head of the professional division of the RWB school, played Drosselmeier, and Marina Eglevsky, daughter of André, was in the lead. But Evelyn Hart stole the opening-night show.

In *The Vancouver Sun* the following day, I led off my review with lengthy praise – for her seemingly instinctive musicality, for her natural, relaxed phrasing, for the poetry and warmth of character that tinged her graceful line, for the cleanliness of her bearing. She was, I suggested, someone to watch.

Sometimes a critic gets lucky. The world has been watching her ever since.

Later, we became friends; she has spent time with my critic-companion Susan Mertens and me at our house beside the ocean in Lions Bay, and from

9

time to time I come across interviews in which she nominates Lions Bay as the place she would like to retire to. She and Mopsa, our Tibetan terrier, exchange postcards.

I have written about her often, always honestly, and yet we have managed to stay friends. Out of that friendship and that regard for what she does on the stage have come this book.

It would not have been possible without Evelyn. I have lost track of the hours we have spent getting everything on the record, mostly over long dinners in restaurants in Winnipeg and Vancouver.

But many other individuals have made significant contributions to the story. Foremost among them are the members of her family, all of whom made me welcome in their homes – her mother, Maxine Hart, and Evelyn's grandmother, Euloeen Edighoffer; her twin sister, Elly, and her husband, Glenn Buckmaster; her brother John and his wife, Kate; her sister Judy, her husband, Sandy Stuart, and their children Luke, whose favourite ballet is Agnes de Mille's cowboy romp, *Rodeo*, Bethanie, who has already begun to dance, and Aaron.

There is also her adopted family in Winnipeg, Lin and Kay Marchbank, their daughter, Cindy, and her husband, Julien Cormier – the people who first gave her a home there – and the members of the Royal Winnipeg Ballet past and present who gave so generously of their time during the research process: Arnold Spohr, John Meehan, Mark Porteous, Lendre Rodgers Kearns, Pamela Anthony, Galina Yordanova, Cathy Taylor, Bill Riske, Earl Stafford, Geoff Hayes, André Lewis, Sarah Slipper, Stephen Hyde, Vincent Boyle, Gino di Marco. Christopher Dafoe's comments were, as always, perceptive.

Beyond Winnipeg, I was fortunate to obtain insights from many members of Evelyn's extended family in the world of dance – most importantly her first teachers, Dorothy and Victoria Carter, in London, Ont.; Reid Anderson, Veronica Tennant, Rex Harrington, Betty Oliphant, and Michael Crabb in Toronto; David Y. H. Lui in Vancouver; Peter Wright and Alexander Grant in London, England; Rudi van Dantzig and Hans van Manen in Amsterdam; Richard Cragun and Marcia Haydée in Stuttgart.

Three of the most significant players in this story are dead – Evelyn's father, Terry Hart, a United Church minister I never met but whose influence permeates these pages; David Peregrine, her medal-winning partner, who became a good friend of mine during the RWB's 1988 tour of the Orient but who was never able to bring himself to give me his side of the story of their troubled relationship; and Henny Jurriens, the Dutch dancer who became artistic director of the RWB. His influence on Evelyn was immense, and he talked to me about her with warmth and insight.

I express my thanks to the Canada Council for the project grant that allowed me to travel to do the necessary research in Canada and Europe, and to my employers at *The Province* in Vancouver for allowing me to take the necessary time.

I am grateful to Dinah Forbes, my editor at McClelland & Stewart, for her careful and thoughtful readings and recommendations, and to Mark Porteous for his close readings of the manuscript.

And once again I express my heartfelt gratitude to Susan Mertens for her support and encouragement, despite extended serious illness, and for her astute commentary and unerring eye. This would not be the same book without her.

M.W.
Lions Bay
April, 1991

DAVID STREET

Evelyn Hart as Valencienne in the National Ballet of Canada's production of The Merry Widow, *choreographed by Ronald Hynd.*

INTRODUCTION

Evelyn Hart's Winnipeg condominium is lit with a sense of drama and decorated like a stage-set. Art overlaps effortlessly into life here, and life into art; there is no easy distinction. It is a reflection of herself.

Her home is her haven, her place of escape, and she admits few. She had lived there a year before she entertained anyone to dinner. Her instinct for perfection in her work is echoed in the attention she paid to the condominium's preparation (new when she bought it, the apartment was substantially and expensively remodelled before she moved in – floors raised, walls removed, doors shifted). She maintains it with a similar meticulousness. When Evelyn's mother and aunt stayed there one Christmas they weren't allowed to leave even a cup in the kitchen sink. When I cooked a meal there once for Evelyn and a small group of her guests, she flustered around for forty-five minutes getting the candles and the placemats right.

The rooms display mementoes from many highpoints in her career – a puppet from her first Romeo, a mask to mark her performance at the Herod Atticus Theatre in Greece, her two Nellies, the "Romeo and Juliet" couch she bought with her proceeds from the television film of the production in which she starred, some *cloisonné* objects from her first trip to China, a rooster doll given to her by Soviet ballerina Nina Ananiashvili when she danced in Moscow, a picture of a rooster from a woman who saw Evelyn being interviewed by Peter Gzowski on TV and sent dolls for both of them, a little mouse from her first roommate, Julie Wilson.

On a tall black pedestal stands a doll in traditional Japanese clothing, presented to her by the head of the technical crew that worked with the Royal Winnipeg Ballet in Japan during the 1988 tour of the Orient ("Thank you Miss Hart for your heart," he wrote. "I admire your dancing but mostly I admire your heart").

Set into the dining table, and dramatically lit from above, is a presentation bowl in red lacquer and mother-of-pearl from the Universal Ballet in Korea. Placed in the bowl, like a flame, is a bright red poppy. Behind the dining table is mounted a large Chinese screen, acquired (like the carpets in the hallway and the bedroom) on tour in Hong Kong. To one side hangs the poster for the 1980 Varna contest that she won – a simple, beautiful image of Alicia Alonso in *Swan Lake*. Evelyn thinks she may one day have her Varna gold medal mounted discreetly at the bottom of the poster. For now, the medals she won in international competition gather dust at the back of her closet.

Her loft bedroom is the only room in the apartment with a window; it gives onto the stained-glass rose window of the church next door. For her first Christmas in the apartment, she decided to illuminate the entire place by candlelight, to enhance the mood of falling snow, the glowing church window across the lane, and the carols on her tape machine; unfortunately, the candles activated the fire detector.

Perhaps the most significant of all the items on display at her home is one of the smallest: a tiny framed postcard, sepia-tinted, of Russian ballerina Anna Pavlova, who in the words of Ruth St. Denis at her memorial service in New York, "lived on the threshold of heaven and earth as an interpreter of the ways of God." If there is a single dancer to whose example Evelyn aspires, it is Pavlova.

Like Pavlova, she is a lyrical, expressive dancer, not a flashy one. She is not a natural trickster. By acting and by dancing she extracts every drop of pathos and passion, yet always manages to hold it back from preposterousness. When she dances she expresses, beyond the technique and the artifice and despite the lights and the costumes, an essence of spontaneity and innocence. Ethereal, spiritual, she shows us the raw, ungovernable centre of her soul.

"It is a charisma," says Stuttgart Ballet director Marcia Haydée. "It has nothing to do with technique, with physicality, with movement – it's something that you're born with." Others echo that view. "There is no dancer in North America to touch you as a total artist," wrote Victoria Carter, Evelyn's teacher, after seeing her dance Juliet. "Someone may have a better *piqué* or pirouette, but there isn't a dancer anywhere in your league for totality:

technique, musicality, phrasing, emotion, line, stagecraft, flow of movement . . . charisma."

Whatever shortcomings there might have been in the area of technique, says Alexander Grant, former artistic director of the National Ballet of Canada, they are far outweighed by the artistry – "and that's what audiences want to see. An artist has an indefinable quality that communicates, and most audiences can put their fingers on it – they saw a performance that knocked them for six, and they will always remember that."

"Most great dancers have a way of subtly breaking the rules," says Reid Anderson, current artistic director of the National Ballet, "so that when you watch them, what they're doing classically is not really pure, from the textbook sense – but that's of course what makes it interesting."

She has (as Cyril Beaumont said Pavlova had) the ability to draw an audience's attention the moment she sets foot on the stage. For the time that she is on the stage, there is no one else to watch; she doesn't enact the fantasy before us – she *is* the fantasy. When the course of action in *Onegin* calls for her to write a letter to her lover, that's what she does. And while she is fully aware of the fact that she is on a stage, she writes the letter in a totally realistic way – "Dear Mr. Onegin, I think you're terrific. What do you think about this, about that?" She even signs the letter "Tatiana," looks at it, and lets the pen fall. "You just have to do it," she says, "just the way you would in your little apartment. It's just a matter of being there."

John Meehan, the Australian *danseur noble* who is now artistic director of the Royal Winnipeg Ballet, remembers how she took over the role of Valencienne in Ronald Hynd's ballet *The Merry Widow*, when she danced it as a guest at the National Ballet of Canada. Meehan, who danced in the original Australian production and staged it in Toronto, recalled how Hynd had taken pains to create a special role for the original Valencienne, Lucette Aldous of the Australian Ballet – "she was in many ways the definitive one. I always measured others against Lucette. But Evelyn was so immediately, completely different that you couldn't begin to compare them. She took that role away from everyone and made it her own."

Veronica Tennant, acclaimed as one of the finest dancers ever produced in Canada, considers Evelyn Hart "one of the most extraordinary ballerinas dancing today, one of the most complete. She has everything that you would wish for and more, esthetically and visually, and then there's such an outpouring of emotion – she uses this extraordinary and pleasing body as an emotional tool. Most other dancers, it balances either way, and they learn to compensate on either one side or the other, but Evelyn is one of those rare, rare creatures who have both in abundance. Her spirit infuses her body.

She has an extraordinary, God-given instrument, but she hasn't stopped at accepting that, she has bent it to the will of man in her way. And then there is so much in her soul and her spirit that she wants to express. There's a bountiful-ness about it, it seems to replenish all the time, and it emanates from every part of the body. Whenever I watch her dance I'm absolutely transported. It's the realization of everyone's dream of what they might hope, and beyond."

"I don't see anyone in the world like her – she's alone," says Galina Yordanova, who mounted *Swan Lake* for the RWB. "There are certain people who are almost born for what they do," says the Dutch choreographer Rudi van Dantzig. "Ulanova was one. It is as if Evelyn is created for dance."

Henny Jurriens, briefly the artistic director of the RWB and the man who, until his untimely death in 1989, was probably the most important single male influence on Evelyn's life after her father, considered her a genius. I remember sitting with him on a Bangkok stage, hidden by a wing-curtain as we watched Evelyn and André Lewis dance Jiří Kylián's lyric-melancholy pas de deux, *Nuages*. The dance fitted her body as naturally as her pale, translucent skin; she looked boneless. Lewis floated her round the stage like a grey cloud. By the end, Jurriens had tears in his eyes. "She is quite, quite remarkable," he said. "We are privileged to be able to work with her."

Not only does she command the admiration and devotion of her peers – fans become effusive in their eagerness to let her know how much she has touched them. "Your *Giselle* will be etched in my mind forever," wrote one Toronto admirer. "I can't count the number of times I've seen *Giselle* but I've NEVER seen anything so beautiful . . . I really wanted to cry and it takes a lot for me to cry." "I felt like a captive slave, experiencing your truly enchanting performance," wrote another. "It was a true artistic creation."

One Vancouver fan wrote: "I can barely breathe as I watch every second, every movement you make. You are to me the most rare and precious of all that true dance is. No other dancer today can come close to you. The whole theatre comes alive with your presence. Thank you for sharing yourself with us. May your soul soar." A Winnipeg admirer wrote of *The Dying Swan* – " . . . it was one of the most beautiful things I have ever seen in my entire life. I have always admired your incredible artistry and to witness that moment was so magical, I couldn't move from my seat. I was numb." She thanked Evelyn, in particular, for the inspiration that her dancing gave her to pursue her own career as a singer.

It is the same internationally. "I was spellbound," wrote an admirer after her 1984 debut in *Swan Lake* with Sadler's Wells Royal Ballet in Cambridge, England. "How about staying with Sadler's Wells?" "Your *Giselle* is very pretty and gentle," wrote an enthusiast in Japan in 1988. "You're the best dancer in

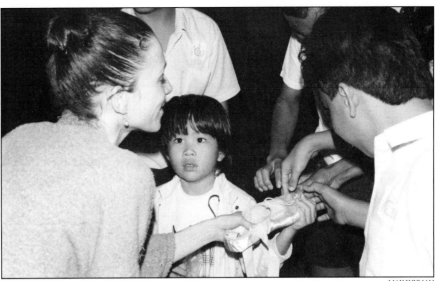

MAX WYMAN

Evelyn shows her shoes to children attending a 1988 matinée in Singapore.

the world . . . Why you are so wonderful dancer!? During I saw your dance, it likes I'm in the dream." Another Japanese girl, in a letter that made Evelyn weep when she received it, wrote: "I like ballet as much as you, but I can't take ballet lessons for some reason. I really envy you. I will support you as much as I can. Please love your ballet. Please don't forget loving ballet even though you go through hardship."

Her response to her fans is equally warm. Some stars sign their names without looking at the recipient, some slip out of a side door of the theatre to avoid having to face the mob. But each autograph-seeker gets a special inscription from Evelyn, and she always has time for them all, even when they number, as they did on tour in Japan, in the hundreds.

She has a particular sympathy for young would-be ballerinas. Sharing the excitement of children, even for a few moments, lets her make up for the things she lost in the trials and tribulations of her own process of becoming a ballerina. Typically, when she appeared on the wish-fulfilment TV show "Thrill of a Lifetime," she went far beyond the needs of the script; a little girl from Fort McMurray who simply wanted to meet a ballerina eventually learned a pas de deux with Evelyn Hart.

Since childhood, the need to dance has consumed her, and she has fought against great odds to fulfil that need. Once when she was suffering a series of severe headaches she dreamed she had a brain tumour. Without an operation the doctor said she had only three weeks to live. With the operation, she had a chance of surviving – but she would never be able to dance again. The dilemma terrified her, and she woke in a panic.

Outside the studio, she lives a life of self-imposed isolation. Her former agent could never get her to answer the phone. When Arnold Spohr was artistic director of the company, it once took him two weeks to make contact with her . . . and that was in Winnipeg. Her lack of contact with her family and friends was a source of unhappiness for years. But that was the way Evelyn preferred it. Dancing filled her days; her drive to dance – the vision of what was possible – was more company than people could provide.

Her sense of isolation is indivisibly intertwined with her urge for perfection. There is no moment in her day when she is not measuring herself against an unattainable ideal. While she has a great capacity for encouragement and inspiration and can make anyone she is with feel extraordinarily close, she can also be difficult and demanding in her work and in her relationships with the people around her. The difficulties arise from her perception of what she needs in order to become the artist she wants to be. Work is paramount. Before a day can begin, she must always have the basics of work organized – class, rehearsal, the right shoes (shoes have always been a problem: once the company flew her to Austria to discuss her needs in person with a Viennese shoemaker). When she went to her uncle's funeral in 1988, she was doing her daily barre exercises in the family living room as the guests were gathering to go to the funeral service.

Evelyn Hart is ready to bleed for her artform. When she had a biopsy to check on a suspicion for breast cancer (unfounded, it turned out) she insisted on going to rehearsal the next day with her drainage tubes still in place. The incision ripped open, and there was blood all over her leotard. When she had her wisdom teeth removed during the rehearsal period for her first *Giselle*, she added a gruesome touch of realism to the mad scene, parting her lips in an agony of anguish to display a mouthful of blood.

She has spent much of her career searching for the perfect partner, in Canada and abroad – a partner who will allow her, as she puts it, to open the trapdoor of her creativity. However, her constant lack of satisfaction with herself inevitably means that – partly through guilt, partly through impossible expectation – she demands far more from her partners than other dancers might. What she seeks is a total giving, an instinctive unanimity without barriers. More often, she has felt "a crystal clear wall" between herself and her partners, "even if he has his head on my cheek."

One of the partnering experiences she valued most was dancing with Anthony Dowell of the Royal Ballet. "It was as though he was dancing *with* me, so I wasn't aware that he was really partnering me – as though his body, even though I couldn't see it, was taking on the same shapes as mine, responding with the same concepts to the music. He's an unbelievably proficient partner, and he brings something out of you on the stage that you're not really expecting. I don't feel *attached*, and yet I feel totally secure. It's not only physical but it's also in the way he hears and phrases the music – when you're dancing with him you don't have to see him to know how close he is to what you're feeling."

Richard Cragun, of the Stuttgart Ballet, is another dancer Evelyn considers a soulmate. He too was ready to listen to her ideas and adjust to her interpretation, and again it was that openness that she gravitated towards. Cragun, for his part, was attracted by her commitment. It was so intense that it demanded from him a modification of his own on-stage persona. "She's like a Stradivarius," he says. "She's such a delicate instrument that to be in any way rough or strong will break it. I would like to think that I have a very sensitive side but it pulled out of me everything I could find of sensivity in order to cope with the person."

Her emphasis on the development of her art, and on the search for the perfect on-stage partner, has taken its toll on her off-stage life. The ballet studio is a place where illusions are prepared; illusions of love. In the ballet studio, two dancers preparing a pas de deux are required to reach a condition in which they can convince an audience that there exists between them the transcendent passion and consuming care of the great romances. To make this possible, the ballet studio allows them to skip many of the preliminaries that mere mortals might suffer through in their progress toward an enduring relationship, and fall in love, or give the impression of falling in love, very quickly.

This can be a very attractive process to experience. If they do this enough times, it can become a habit. But it can have disastrous effects when applied to relationships outside the charmed world of the studio or the theatre. Evelyn has always found it inhibiting. "I go right from point A to point Z . . . then all of a sudden I go, *oops!* It's the intensity of the theatre, spoiling it. And it's so hard when you've had that experience on-stage – it's really spiritual, not just physical or intellectual – because to achieve that between two people takes a long time in everyday life."

It follows then that her closest friends tend to be dancers. Henny Jurriens was the closest of them all. Although she has in recent years been able to develop a circle of friends who recognize that her commitment is first to her work, and enjoy her and accept her without the conventional expectations of thank-you notes and casual phone calls, it was not until she met Jurriens that she found a man who was able to be a fully accepting, fully understanding

MAX WYMAN

Evelyn deep in conversation with Henny Jurriens on the "bullet" train between Tokyo and Osaka, 1988.

friend. The relationship Evelyn forged with him transcended the professional. What evolved between them was a curious mixture of almost-marriage, friendship, soul-entwining. He was the first person in whom she felt confident enough to place her absolute trust. He was also the first person whom she felt really understood her, understood that the stage was the only place where she was truly happy, deep within her soul. On tour they would spend hours together, sitting in a corner or snuggled down in adjoining seats on trains or planes, talking about life, talking about love. "It's the first male relationship that has made me grow, because of his understanding of who I am," she told me in 1988. So while she realizes that staying on at the RWB when Jurriens took over as artistic director in 1988 may not have been her wisest career move, it was perhaps inevitable – the ultimate intermingling of affection and art. "I wanted to let him know I was part of his vision," she says. "I would have given anything for the company and his dream to succeed. That was the closest I came to being married – I was married to his dream."

Her resistance to making a full commitment to a relationship also has to do with the type of career she has chosen. Certain conditions of being a dancer get in the way of any relationship outside the theatre. Dancers are of necessity independent, and often ambitious. While they are high-strung and sensitive about their art, their egos are healthily developed. In the case of an individual like Evelyn, there is also a fire to their creative determination that makes them hard to live with. All these are factors that demand an understanding that is often hard to find beyond the theatre's protective walls.

But in Evelyn's case, even these problems dwindle to insignificance beside the more important question of personal commitment. Simply put, relationships take second place to her work. She values her freedom too much – freedom to look at the world as an adult one moment, a child the next, freedom to explore her personal interior for her art.

She is not unaware of the joys she is missing. Being in love, she says, puts her in touch with another side of herself. It changes the tenor of her day. Life in general seems to become easier. But she says, only half-joking, that she thinks she is probably "unlivable with." The stage allows her to make a fool of herself, put her feelings on the line, but off-stage her shyness and insecurity make that virtually impossible.

"It's a way of settling the way I want to live," she says. "It's literally having to share your space with someone else. I don't trust someone with my heart very easily. I have come to the realization that I'm not in the slightest bit interested in having family, children, husband, lover – I really couldn't care less. What you need, I tell myself, is good professional friends you can lean on and people you can talk to. But don't kid anyone. You love your independence."

And she loves her independence, of course, because it frees her for the strongest and most fulfilling relationship of all, her relationship with her work.

"You have to spend the time to create a trusting relationship, and every day I don't let my work down creates a stronger bond. I stick with it because I love it, I cherish it, I respect it – it is a creature, a being, it has a life, and you become one with it, and the more you commit yourself and give yourself to it and hold it with respect and integrity the more you can relax and the more it grows."

The twin girls, aged four, in the garden behind the manse at Port Credit.

MAXINE HART

1 *"Is She a Dancer?"*

*M*axine Hart was convinced she was carrying twins. Every time she went to the doctor for a check-up, she was sure she would come home to her husband Terry with the news that they were going to add two more children to the son and daughter they already had – but every time, the doctor said no, she was carrying just one big baby.

When the pregnancy was well-advanced, the doctor said he thought Maxine was putting on too much weight, and told her to diet. She did.

Three weeks later, at St. Michael's Hospital, Toronto, she bore twin girls – "premature, we thought about two months," says Maxine, "but we'll never know. With me cutting down on the food and so on, we were lucky that they were . . ." Her voice trails away at the memory.

Evelyn Anne was born first, at 9:12 on the morning of April 4, 1956. She was the smaller of the two, at four pounds twelve ounces. She was kept in hospital for two weeks until she was considered strong enough to go home. Her twin, Eleanor Jane, born four minutes later, weighed five pounds three ounces. She stayed in hospital a week.

We are all shaped, to a greater or lesser degree, by our beginnings. And in Evelyn Hart's case her family made her. Her private fears and her self-doubt as well as her public successes and her much-acclaimed expressive artistry are rooted in her early family life. Her life since she broke away from her family and began her career in dancing has, in a sense, been one long coming-to-terms with its immense influence.

Mother, father, siblings – twin sister in particular – their influences resonate through Evelyn's life and work like siren calls; irresistible, dangerous, significant. Here, in the musicality, spirituality, and selfless commitment of her father, a church minister, lie the origins of her artistry and dedication. Here, in her mother's protective opposition to the idea of dancing as a career, lie the origins of her self-doubt and her need to punish her body for its imagined failures. Here, in her instinctive competitiveness with her twin, lie the origins of her superhuman application to the brute task of making her dancing better.

The influence of Terry and Maxine Hart on their family was inevitably and indelibly an influence rooted in the teachings of the church. Church figured prominently in the lives of the children – Sunday services, Sunday school, CGIT (Canadian Girls in Training) for the girls. The religious influence permeated their entire existence. The children were trained from their earliest years to have compassion, understanding, and tolerance of others, and it seemed to them that they had to obey more rules than other kids. Their friends did things on Sunday afternoon that they weren't allowed to do because they weren't proper activities for a Sunday. If people were shown kissing on the television, Terry would turn it off. Dirty jokes were a genuine embarrassment – Elly had a terrible time one summer coping as camp counsellor for a cabin of twelve-year-old boys. And of course, no smoking, no drinking.

They learned by instruction, by example, and by osmosis. When Evelyn, in a fit of temper, told her father one day that she hated him, he told her calmly

MAXINE HART

Seventeen months old, Evelyn crawls along Bayfield Beach on Lake Huron during family holidays in the summer of 1957.

that she did not hate anyone. "Most parents are concerned about your physical or emotional health," she says. "My father was concerned about our spiritual health."

The family itself is a tight, mutually supportive cocoon, and Evelyn's implicit rejection of its protective casing, in favour of an environment that would allow her artistry to flower, has been an enduring source of hurt and disappointment for all. Virtually the only times the family has been together as a unit in the years since she moved to Winnipeg to begin her dancing career have been times of bereavement – her father's death in 1976, her uncle's death in 1988. Christmas, a time of great significance and celebration for this church-oriented family, is always incomplete in her mother's eyes because Evelyn is never there. The demands of her work meant she missed the weddings of all three of her siblings. When her sister Elly began to train in psychiatry, the class was asked one day to draw family pictures. Elly drew a circle of people, with one person outside the circle – Evelyn far away in Winnipeg.

Part of this estrangement from the family may be a deliberate distancing from things that were – and are still – painful to her, particularly her difficult relationship with her mother, Maxine; a gulf of guilt separated mother and daughter for years. Part of it is the simple fact (a fact they all recognize) that she has developed interests and obsessions that they are unable to share at her level of intensity. Of course they are proud of her and what she has done, but that is something that exists somewhere outside. They wish her well. But they miss her.

Maxine Hart was born Maxine Anne Edighoffer on January 7, 1927, at the general hospital in Stratford, a quiet southern Ontario town that has become internationally famous as the home of the Stratford Festival. She was brought up in Mitchell, a town of about 2,500, thirteen miles northwest of Stratford. Welcome to Mitchell, says a roadside sign as you approach the community, A Pleasant Place To Live.

Edighoffer's general store, on Mitchell's Main Street, was established by Maxine's grandfather, taken over by her father, then by her brother, and is currently operated by her nephew, Robert. This is the place to which the Edighoffers return; Maxine lives today with her mother, Euloeen Edighoffer, in a low, handsome house her parents built. It was their dream home, modelled on Frank Lloyd Wright's principles of harmony with the landscape, the first house in Mitchell to have electricity. In winter, Maxine, a fitness enthusiast, can ski from the front door. (This is an active family; at age ninety-two, Euloeen was still going out regularly in the afternoons to play shuffleboard with her friends.) Maxine's sister Mary lives in the house next door. A couple of streets away live their aunt and uncle; nearby, their brother and his wife. This is where Maxine brought her husband and children for family get-togethers. From the age of two, Evelyn played dress-up in the children's clothing department at the family store.

Terrence (Terry) Victor Hart was born in Toronto on February 16, 1910. His mother was an immigrant from Northern Ireland; members of the family still live at Ballymartin, near Newry in County Down. His father's family grew up in poverty near Lindsay, Ontario, the children walking seven miles a day to school. Terry's father was the first member of the family to break free of the cycle of poverty; he established a career for himself as a druggist in Toronto.

The family was a religious one but had no history of service to the church. However, when Terry was sixteen, he promised his mother on her deathbed that he would enter the ministry of the United Church. He subsequently pursued his vocation with the same kind of single-mindedness that was to consume the rest of his life.

He had studiousness thrust upon him. Short of stature, he was always the youngest-looking person in his class, with a physical frailty that barred him from competitive sports or extreme physical activity (one of his greatest disappointments was being turned down for physical reasons in his bid to become a missionary in China). He became a bookworm – a lifetime student. Later in life when the family went to the cottage for the summer, the children would pack their flippers and sports equipment and Terry would pack a big box of books. He had a desk at the cottage where he would sit and work all day, and it would take all the wiles of the children to get him out for a half-hour swim.

As a student at Victoria College at the University of Toronto, Terry Hart wrote an essay that won him a scholarship for a year's study at Cambridge University in England. While he was at Cambridge he made a holiday trip by bicycle to his mother's relatives in Ireland – he was considered the unattached bachelor of the family, so it was his obligation to visit them – and those connections have been maintained by Maxine and the children.

He subsequently took theological training at Emmanuel College, Toronto, and was ordained in 1935. During the Second World War he served for four years in the Canadian army, at one point living in Holland with a Dutch pastor and his family at Eelde, and sharing a single room with them when the house was taken over by occupying Nazi forces. Again, Maxine and her family have remained in touch with Terry's Dutch friends.

Maxine and Terry Hart met in 1948, shortly after he had moved to a posting at Kirkland Lake in Northern Ontario. He was thirty-eight, well-established in

Maxine and
Terry Hart
were married
in Kirkland Lake,
Ontario,
on September 20,
1950.

COURTESY MAXINE HART

his calling. Maxine was twenty-one, freshly graduated as a physical education teacher from the University of Toronto. She had just arrived in Kirkland Lake for her first job, teaching at the local high school. She spent her Sundays looking after the girls' class at Sunday school and helping out with the CGIT youth group, another Edighoffer family tradition.

Before Terry Hart arrived at Kirkland Lake to take up his new ministry there had been a lot of talk about this handsome new bachelor who was coming to the neighbourhood, and the knowledgeable money was on one of the more mature church lovelies as the lady most likely to snare him.

But Maxine somehow managed to whip him away from beneath their noses. It was love at first sight – he saw her coming down the aisle leading the CGIT and decided she was the one who was going to be his wife. Their bond from the beginning was their common love of the church, and when after a two-year courtship they were married, he made it clear to her that his work would take precedence over everything.

"He told me, 'Now, you've got to remember that I'll first be married to the church,'" recalls Maxine. "And I came to know what that meant. It meant that I was the parent, responsible for the home and the family – and there was this marvellous person influencing our lives all the time."

United Church ministers rarely stay in a single community for more than a handful of years. Terry and Maxine Hart left Kirkland Lake in 1954 and moved to a small church in Birchcliff, in the east end of Toronto, so Terry could be near his aged father. By this time, they had two children: John, born on August 26, 1951, and Judy, born on April 21, 1953.

Two years later they moved to a much larger church in Port Credit, just west of Toronto. It was during their stay here that the twin girls were born. Five years after that, in 1961, the family moved to Peterborough, Ontario, and in 1970 they moved once again, to Dorchester, a small town about twelve kilometres east of the southern Ontario city of London. This was Terry Hart's last ministry. By the time he died in 1976 at the age of sixty-six, he had completed what was then the standard United Church service period of forty years, with an additional year of part-time service as a church visitor added for good measure. "He literally died on the job," says Maxine.

As a child, Evelyn only had eyes for her father. Soon after beginning dance classes, she discovered how Anna Pavlova had travelled the world to introduce ballet to audiences who had never seen it before. Evelyn was entranced. *That* was who she wanted to be, because that would kill two birds with one stone – she could do what she wanted to do, which was dance, but she could also make her father happy by being a missionary and dancing for all the people in all the countries he had never been able to go to. "Plus," she argued, "it would also be really good in the book of the big man upstairs."

She used to call her father "the big black ghost." She loved the ceremony and theatricality as he came down the aisle in his gown and his tabs. The Christmas Eve candlelight services were best, particularly in the big, beautiful old George Street church in Peterborough – candles in every window and on every ledge, holly boughs, Christmas trees with lights, the singing of the choir, the grandeur of the organ, the procession of gowns sweeping down the aisle . . . she always found it a profoundly moving experience.

And it is her father she credits with the inspiration for her own intensity of communication.

In the United Church, the only times the worshipper kneels on a bench are at confirmation at the age of thirteen – essentially, the moment of admission to the church – and at marriage. Evelyn still vividly remembers the moment her father confirmed her. The memory of the way his voice trembled at the laying-on of hands still brings back tears – an emotional response that derives from "the passion that he communicated, a passion about what he believed in, this sense of hope – of beauty in mankind's spirit and in our world, which I think is related to the spirituality that people see in what I do. He had the ability to communicate thoughts and feelings and emotions through his voice. When I walk in the autumn and I see the leaves, for instance, their beauty just fills my soul – and it's much the same as listening to my father's voice when he preached. The only other person I've heard speak who touched me and moved me in that way was Pierre Trudeau. He communicated the same passion and commitment, the sense that when he spoke it came from the deepest part of his soul."

There are other parallels between father and daughter. He had a well-developed sense of humour, he gave the impression of being at home in a crowd, he loved playing the piano at informal gatherings (John Hart believes that if his father had turned his mind to music as a profession, he could have been a concert pianist), and he never had any trouble preaching – he felt it was his forte. His sense of ecclesiastical theatricality and the need for passionate communication with his flock led him to use a voice for the church that was quite different from the voice he used in normal conversation. But deep down he was shy and insecure. And in that dichotomy between public appearance and private reality, between the appearance of confident control and the fact of inner insecurity, Terry Hart and Evelyn had much in common.

Evelyn also believes much of her obsessiveness about work comes from her father. He would stay at the church for hours; it was his calling and he would not have considered doing anything else. She believes it was from that example that she drew her determination to succeed and her courage to remain steadfast in her commitment to her art, no matter what.

In the same way she has inherited her father's sense of obligation to others without thought of personal gain. She has often said that she dances not for what she can get, but for what she can give. She is moved by her awareness of a gift that she is able to share.

Inevitably, the children went through periods of resistance to their parents' religious emphasis. They were growing up at a time and in a society in which a church minister's family had certain social responsibilities without receiving many of society's material benefits, and the deprivations turned them – in a decorous, minister's-children sort of way – rebellious. John, for instance, went through a phase where he would deliberately cause trouble, getting into confrontations with his mother over small matters like washing the dishes. He had three sisters; if they were good for anything at all, they were good for washing the dishes. Maxine didn't see it that way. She hit him over the head with a frying-pan.

After he left home at eighteen he had little to do with the church until he settled down and married in London, Ontario, though he believes the influence of an upbringing of that kind can never be escaped. "I always thought of my father as a good man," he says, "the kind of man who – regardless of whether you drive a train or are a minister – if you can live your life the way he did, that's basically the right way to do it." He eventually became chairman of his church. He and his wife, Kate, named their firstborn, a boy, after Terry Hart.

Evelyn's move away from the church happened at the age of seventeen, when she began her studies in Winnipeg. Until that time, she had attended every Sunday without question. Even when they were at their summer cottage, Terry would pack them off to church at nearby Dunsford. It was a duty. Evelyn used to hate it. She says now she only became confirmed to make her father happy.

Unlike her father, who one year resolved to lock himself in his study and read the Bible from cover to cover and then did, she doesn't study the Bible at all – though she believes that its principles are deeply instilled in her and function as guidelines for her life. Nor does she go to church, except on the rare occasions when she is with her family. She believes religion functions principally as a moral guideline – "the goal is to be as generous, as warm, as human, as intelligent a human being as possible. And in a sense, for me, ballet replaces religion, in that it involves commitment and integrity and honesty and discipline. It's not that ballet *is* a religion; but that sense of discipline, family, community . . . you get that from ballet, too."

Even so, her early experience of the church gives her a contemplative bent. In conversation, she will speculate on the possibilities of a former life, of an afterlife, and of reincarnation.

"Haven't you ever done something that you just knew how to do, or met someone you immediately felt you had known all your life?" she asks. "Why is it that sometimes you meet someone who has nothing to do with your career, you don't necessarily even like the person, but you fall in love? There's no reason for you to love the person; they may be irresponsible, abrasive, completely from a different background. You have nothing in common, but you feel there's just something there. You're not able to explain it but it just haunts you. I often wonder if they're people you have known in previous lives, and you're destined not to get along."

Her church upbringing taught her to believe in an afterlife, and she returns to the evidence of her senses (the realization, for instance, that, once he had died, her father's body was just so much inert substance, cold to the touch, "an exact replica of what he was when he was alive, but lacking the soul, which was unpredictable, spontaneous, warm, encompassing, embracing, that made him that special human being") to support the thought that some kind of eternal spirit exists in every human creature. "When we see that

Family Christmas at the manse in Port Credit, Ontario: the twins aged about three, are seated at the front, with John and Judy behind them.

COURTESY MAXINE HART

someone's spirit has left them it's much more possible to believe that the spirit lives on and doesn't die . . . so you think, why shouldn't there be the possibility of coming back to learn more lessons?"

She regards prayer as a form of communication with a greater force – "though, as the church says about God's will, you can pray for something, but that doesn't necessarily mean that it's going to help. I do think there is a connection, but I think we have to know how. In a sense you have to dedicate your life to that communication, just the way you dedicate your life to ballet – and if you're not comfortable with it, of course it's not going to work."

She danced her first solo with the Royal Winnipeg Ballet the night her father died, in October 1976. Later the same night, she woke in a panic, her heart pounding. She had been dreaming that her father was falling – "he kept falling for several minutes, then all of a sudden Jesus Christ stepped out and caught him and started walking upwards with him. And I was absolutely calm from that instant; and I went to sleep."

Her father has appeared to her often in her dreams since then, usually at significant moments in her life. When she was in Japan in 1980, taking part in the international dance competition in Osaka, she had a dream in which she saw her father and her grandfather walking arm-in-arm in a garden. "They both had books under their arms. It was a beautiful garden but I couldn't make out any detail." The next day she learned her grandfather had died.

In 1988 she was on tour with the Royal Winnipeg Ballet, again in Japan. Tokyo audiences adore her, and it was she, not the company, who was getting top billing on the posters for *Giselle*. Evelyn was terrified. The night before opening, she dreamed she was on a train with her mother. Her mother was playing a tape-recording that she said was the voice of Evelyn's father. Evelyn knew it wasn't but some time later, as she rose from the dream to consciousness, she felt a breeze touch her lips – a breeze that she swore was her father.

The next day Henny Jurriens wrote her a note before the opening performance, saying he realized that she felt insecure because she didn't think she deserved the talent she had, but telling her he believed her father would have wanted her to go ahead. It was almost, she felt, as if her father had been there in the night and persuaded Henny to write the note.

Maxine Hart's moral influence on Evelyn had always been there. She is a devout churchwoman, keen on the concept of service to others. In Peterborough she spent time working with alcoholics, and her children are warm in their praise of her courageous stance in defence of homosexuals during the United Church furore over their acceptance into the church ministry. (Ironically, it was her encounters with homosexuals in the ballet world through Evelyn that brought her to this understanding – a stance that led to her being ostracized by fellow churchgoers in Mitchell.)

She encouraged the children to be good to others and to appreciate natural beauty (she would make John slow down when he was driving her between towns on country roads because "you're driving too fast – I can't see the beauty around here"). She also influenced the children in their attitudes to eating, stressing health foods, banning sweet cereals, and experimenting with natural additives. She continues to work consciously to do as little damage as possible to the world she lives in, conserving water, recycling whatever she can, and eating very little meat. "I guess I would be quite happy if everyone was on a diet," she says.

The influence of Evelyn Hart's siblings on her is evident in more subtle ways.

Judy clearly remembers when the twin girls were born because they were premature. "I remember people coming to the house and patting John on the head, patting me on the head, and making for the nursery – 'So, where are they?'" Inevitably, the babies got most of the attention; inevitably, there was sibling jealousy. Evelyn and Judy have never been particularly close.

John never thought that he liked his sisters much. There were three of them and one of him, and what *he* really wanted was a brother. So he would torment them whenever he could, chasing them around the house, pinning them down and tickling them, Elly in particular – she called it "death by tickling."

Elly was the tomboy of the twins, and liked rambunctiousness. John didn't trap and tickle Evelyn as often – she had more of a temper and wouldn't have tolerated it as well. He remembers her too as "a very obstinate kid. If she thought she was right, it wouldn't have mattered even if the Pope had called up and said 'Evelyn, you're wrong' – she would have said, 'Okay, but I know *you're* wrong.'"

A single example of that stubbornness: the twins started taking French when they were in Grade 4, by which time John had done several years of high-school French. So when Evelyn came home one day and told him he was a "gasson," he was able to correct her. "I said, 'No, you mean *garçon*.' She said 'No, gasson; you're a gasson.' I said 'No, there's an r in it – it's *garçon*.' She said 'No, there is no r in it.' And she was absolutely convinced. I got a dictionary and showed her; she still said no."

Their home life was warm and sheltered (John says he learned more about life in the first year he was away from home at university than he had in the previous eighteen). They were never taken to art galleries, and since money was tight, rarely to the cinema. The only movies Evelyn remembers seeing during her childhood are *My Fair Lady*, *The Sound of Music*, and *Mary Poppins*. On rainy days, they would put on little shows at the manse to entertain each other. They did some amateur dramatics (Judy, who still acts, won high marks in drama festivals) and in high school Evelyn played one of the blind children in *The Miracle Worker* (she felt thoroughly insulted by the role, convinced she should have been Helen Keller) and auditioned for the lead role of Maria in a production of *The Sound of Music* (another insult – she got the show's only non-singing role, Frau Schmidt, the housekeeper).

Principally, though, music dominated their days. It was an integral part of daily existence. While other kids in the neighbourhood were listening to the top ten on the radio, the Hart household hits were Beethoven and Mendelssohn. When Evelyn was ten, her favourite music was Beethoven's *Eroica*.

All four children took piano lessons in Peterborough with a Miss Harstone, who had a studio in a big old house near the manse. The children worked out among themselves a program that would allow each of them to get in his or her piano practice each day, although they often found themselves competing for piano time with their father, whose preferred means of relaxing after work was to play favourite classical piano compositions. They all competed at the local music festivals, Evelyn and Elly often playing piano duets together.

Both girls also played the violin when they were young. Elly played from Grades 6 to 9, and made it into the Peterborough Youth Orchestra as a regular

MAXINE HART

The musical Hart children: left to right, Judy, John, Evelyn, and Elly, at the family home at Peterborough in the mid-1960s.

player. Evelyn played in the orchestra for one performance. Initially, great things were prophesied for her, and Maxine arranged special coaching from a private teacher in Peterborough, but Elly scored better on a couple of tests, and Evelyn promptly quit.

The competitiveness among the four children was intense. John was an honours student, Judy was always bringing home trophies for academic subjects, and Evelyn was determined to keep up the family name. "I considered Elly absolutely stupid," she says. "She never made less than a B-plus average, but I'm sure she was totally intimidated. And since I almost always had better marks than she did, it stopped being a competition." Elly believes that the fact they were always in the same class was a big mistake. For a year, in Grade 6, they were separated, and Elly began to pick up rapidly. Then they were put together again and she slipped back.

Even so, they played together, went biking together, took piano and swimming lessons together. On their birthday they had twin cakes with reversed-colour icing – yellow with purple trim, purple with yellow trim. The year they turned thirteen Maxine took them out of school for the day and they went into downtown Peterborough for a meal and a shopping trip: she had made them babydoll dresses for their birthday, and she bought them kneesocks to match the stripes in them. Kneesocks and skipping-ropes.

Christmas was always a big event, with Terry playing the piano for family carols, and everyone involved in acting charades. Evelyn was usually the first awake on Christmas morning. She would wake Elly and they would tiptoe downstairs before anyone else was up to check their Christmas stockings, opening their presents, then rewrapping them and sneaking back upstairs, trying to make it look like a surprise when the gifts were distributed to the gathered family later in the morning.

The two girls didn't have many friends. They didn't need them – they had each other. For most of their childhood they shared the same bedroom, and they'd sneak their light on after everyone had gone to bed and make up songs together, Elly singing a line, Evelyn singing a line. Whenever the family moved to a new community each twin had the comfort of a friend her own age in her new home.

Gradually, however, differences between the twin girls became apparent. Evelyn would go to school half an hour early, Elly would go half an hour late. Elly was happy being a twin, Evelyn hated it – she wanted to be independent. Maxine dressed them the same. Evelyn hated it, Elly loved it. Later, Elly used to wait until Evelyn had dressed for school, then go and change into the same outfit. It infuriated Evelyn.

Differences of temperament began to emerge. Each girl had her own dolls, with their own clothes, and made sure they didn't mix. "She had a little bride doll," says Elly. "It was her favourite. I was so mad at her one day I cut the veil – I put a little snip in it. She was mad for such a long time. I felt awful. It was *the* worst thing you could possibly do."

Most important of all, in terms of their diverging future, differences of attitude began to arise. Evelyn liked to dress up in pretty, lacy things. Elly hated lace. When they watched *The Nutcracker* on television at Christmas, Elly wanted to be one of the boy dancers, leaping around; Evelyn wanted to play one of the glamorous parts. When they played dress-up games, Evelyn was always the bride or the princess, wearing a hat and feathers and a beautiful dress; Elly was always the groom, in one of Terry's old jackets.

These games didn't mean that Evelyn wanted to get married, she just loved the beauty of the clothes and the jewellery and the ceremony of walking down the aisle of a church filled with flowers. No one else was involved in these fantasies. Her favourite scene from the movies, and one that she says still brings her to tears, is Julie Andrews walking down the aisle in *The Sound of Music*. Her parents often took her to weddings at the church when she was young, and her favourite photo album to pore over on wet evenings was the album of her parents' wedding pictures. These images have stayed vividly in her mind – "I thought my mother had such good taste. Her dress was cream velvet with a little collar and a little vee, with gathers all around the skirt, and it came into a train at the back. And she wore a beautiful headpiece: nothing

*Twin
twenty-first
birthday cakes
for the
twin girls,
April 4,
1977.*

COURTESY MAXINE HART

with jewels, just with flowerets, buds of flowers, very small, in a three-quarters wreath around her head. She saved her gown for me."

To be a bride or a princess – that was her childish dream. She fantasized often about being part of the royal family. When she was eight she had romantic dreams of breaking away from that life and becoming a peasant – "but really," she says, "I wanted to be a princess more than life itself."

Elly, meanwhile, was becoming more and more of a tomboy. And gradually, as their interests began to diverge, the girls began to drift apart. Elly began to spend more time with John and Judy than she did with Evelyn. And Evelyn began to spend more and more time with the ballet.

The family was still living in Peterborough when Evelyn had her first crucial exposure to the expressive power of dancing. It was Norman Campbell's 1966 CBC television version of the National Ballet of Canada's production of John Cranko's *Romeo and Juliet*, with Veronica Tennant in the lead. Evelyn was ten, and the experience changed her life. "I realized I had never seen anything quite so beautiful. I didn't know what it was, but it was beautiful."

A neighbour who had taught ballet in her younger years gave the child an old pink-and-blue tutu that came to her knees, and she would dance around the living room in it, often sneaking down the stairs late in the evening when her father was relaxing at the piano to improvise as he played.

She started to nag her mother to take out books on ballet from the Peterborough Public Library, and Maxine would bring her books on Markova, Ulanova, and Plisetskaya. Evelyn had no idea who they were, and didn't care; it wasn't the text she was interested in, it was the pictures – because that was what being a ballerina was all about. She even cut out the ballerinas from the plastic wrap on the Ballet brand of toilet tissue and pasted them in her scrapbook.

The following year, a group of dancers from the National Ballet School, headed by school director Betty Oliphant, visited Peterborough to give a lecture-demonstration for the Women's Art Association in the basement of Trinity United Church. Maxine was invited to attend by a friend, and by now well aware of her daughter's obsession, took Evelyn out of school for the afternoon so she could go with her.

After the presentation Maxine took Evelyn to meet Betty Oliphant to ask about lessons. Evelyn was wearing her brown winter coat and had put her hair up for the occasion.

"Is she a dancer?" asked Oliphant.

"Oh, no, no, no," said Maxine.

"Well," said Oliphant, "she *looks* like one."

That was the turning point. Until now Evelyn had just been one more ballet-crazed little girl. But those words struck some deep chord. Betty Oliphant thought she *looked* like a dancer? Then she was going to become one.

She pestered her parents to get her an audition at the National Ballet School. She wanted to take ballet and she wanted to take it now. Her enthusiasm was to lead to her first huge disappointment.

Evelyn at practice in her early years in the company.

DAVID COOPER

2 EH Loves BP

*T*he lecture-demonstration had set Evelyn's imagination aflame. Eventually, Maxine agreed to write to the National Ballet School to ask for an audition. Evelyn still has the letter confirming the audition appointment, typed in brown ink on NBS letterhead. She was eleven, with no formal dance training of any kind.

A neighbour whose daughter was already attending the school was planning a visit on the date of the audition and she agreed to drive Evelyn from Peterborough to Toronto. In its instructions to candidates, the school suggested that if they had no leotard or tights they bring a swimsuit. Evelyn had no ballet costume – it was not something the minister's salary could manage – so she took along her swimsuit, though she was dreading having to wear it. To her relief, the neighbour was able to loan Evelyn some pink tights and a black leotard. No one had shoes that were small enough to fit her, so she auditioned in little navy-blue socks.

All the other candidates had had ballet training. When she walked into the audition room, some of them were sitting in the splits, looking to her child's eye like perfect little ballerinas; at least one of them was eventually taken into the National Ballet company. One was wearing a costume that looked like a bathing-suit, and Evelyn, on impulse, went to her and began to commiserate – "*I* was going to have to wear a bathing-suit too" – trying to make her feel comfortable. When the girl informed Evelyn with some dignity that what she was wearing was not a bathing-suit but a ballet costume, Evelyn was chagrined.

The results of the audition were equally painful. She didn't know a step of formal ballet, and while she has wiped from her memory the details of the things she did, the memory of the letter of rejection is ineradicably etched – "although we cannot accept your daughter, there is nothing wrong with her body; it is just not fitted for ballet . . . we hope she will maintain her interest in ballet and follow it as a hobby."

The rejection, painful as it was, simply reinforced her determination to become a dancer.

The Peterborough Women's Art Association had given a scholarship to a local girl, Wanda Ross, for studies at the National Ballet School, on condition that she come home on weekends and teach. Evelyn persuaded her parents to let her take these classes at the Peterborough YWCA.

Although she says now that the teaching she was given at that time was not sufficient to give her a firm footing in ballet technique, it was enough to win her a place when she was thirteen in the National Ballet School's summer session. She hoped this would be followed by her acceptance into the school that fall, but again she was turned down because of her lack of training.

However, Evelyn did meet someone that summer who later had a crucial influence on her career. Victoria Carter was an apprentice teacher at the Toronto school, and she remembers being impressed immediately by this intense child. "I couldn't understand why the school didn't accept her," she recalls. "I thought she was fabulous. She wasn't very knowledgeable, and she had very little training, but she had this beautiful body, this wonderful mind, and she was so musical."

Victoria Carter was from London, Ontario. Her mother, Dorothy Carter, had emigrated to Canada in 1955 from Doncaster, England, where her parents operated a thriving dance school. Gradually she built a dance-teaching business of her own, and today Dorothy and Victoria Carter operate a school of about three hundred students in London. It was the Carters who proved to be the early salvation of Evelyn Hart – though not without a fight.

In 1970, when the twins were fourteen, Terry Hart was called to the ministry in Dorchester, a community of less than 2,000 near London, Ontario. Dorchester United Church is a handsome beige brick building that celebrated its centenary in 1989. When Terry Hart was minister, the congregation numbered about two hundred, not all of them active. Evelyn and Elly did their best to be charming and sympathetic and play the proper role of minister's

*Evelyn
at the barre
in the
"hallowed halls"
of the Carter
studio in
London, Ontario,
1972.*

VICTORIA CARTER

children, but coming from a much larger church in what was by comparison a big city, they found it hard to take the new church seriously. They disgraced themselves at their father's induction service by getting a fit of the giggles and exploding into barely suppressed snorts of laughter at the off-key singing of the elderly members of the choir.

The family lived across from the church in an imposing brick manse. Evelyn's room at the top of the house had floral print wallpaper in a pattern of Greek urns with pink and blue flowers and little garlands. The curtains were yellow, the floor was linoleum. The headboard of the bed (supplied, like other items of furniture, by the church) had finely decorated dowels. With its attic and its dark staircases, it was a fine house for nightmares; scared to be there alone at night, fearful of the killer she was sure lurked in the basement, Evelyn had terrifying dreams of stabbing and blood, fires and witchcraft.

Her determination to become a dancer had now become a full obsession. When the family moved from Peterborough to Dorchester, Maxine asked the teachers at the National Ballet School to recommend a local instructor. They suggested the Carter school in London, and Maxine duly phoned for an appointment. Victoria Carter, back in London in partnership with her mother, remembered the child from the previous summer's session in Toronto, and arrangements were made for her to audition for the school.

From Evelyn's point of view, that initial audition class was not encouraging. "They asked me to do an *entrechat quatre*," she recalls, "and I think they must have been horrified at how I did it. Dorothy asked if someone had taught it to me or if I had learned it myself, because I'd been picking up all the ballet books

I could, and I said I'd learned it myself, and you could see it in her eyes, going, 'I should have known it.'"

After that preliminary class, the Carters travelled to Dorchester to talk to Maxine about her daughter's future in dance. Evelyn crept down the hall to eavesdrop at the partly opened door. She remembers hearing them say it would be something of a risk, but they took her anyway, and by the fall of 1970 she was attending several classes a week.

John Hart believes that it was the Carters' decision to take her on as a student that brought about everything that followed; without the Carters, Evelyn would never have been able to fulfil her aim. Evelyn agrees. "They are indelibly etched on my soul for life. Without them I wouldn't be where I am. To this day I attribute my whole being in dance to those two women. It is because of the Carters that I am a dancer."

There was initially some thought that her involvement in the school would be merely recreational, but it soon became evident that this was a more than ordinary talent. The Carters' rambling old house on the corner of leafy St. George and Sydenham streets became Evelyn's second home. She loved the school's air of tradition, memorized the ballet photographs on the wall, and soaked up the atmosphere of the rehearsal studio. She called the building "the hallowed halls."

Most important, she found the beginning of her solid formal training. Most other girls of her age with serious ambitions in dance had already been in intense study for several years; Evelyn was acutely aware of how much catching-up she had to do. The Carters had the challenge of taking raw talent and giving it a framework of technique. They began with things as simple as the five positions of the feet.

What they also provided – and what made it easy for her to accept their technical help – was a recognition and an acceptance of her instinct and love for dance artistry and theatricality. She believes that from the start they understood her soul, but they also knew that she needed the practical means to express it. Almost by accident, she had fallen into an ideal circumstance. The Carters were the means to make her dream come true. They were her escape. They saw the talent, but they also recognized her desire, her absolute need to dance.

It was the manner of the time for teachers to remain somewhat aloof from their charges, and the Carters have never been women to play favourites or to fawn over talent. Their job, as they see it, is to facilitate its emergence. Much later, Victoria Carter wrote to Evelyn: "I often wanted to tell you how good you were, what magnificent potential you had – but when you do, often people feel it will happen and don't go through the work and pain it takes to reach their potential. When you feel assured something will happen you don't always chase after it with the fibre and desperate purpose needed to achieve it."

So they kept their own counsel, although it rapidly became clear that Evelyn had both fibre and desperate purpose in abundance. Her rate of progress was phenomenal. "You never had to teach her a second time," says Victoria Carter. "She had an eye that could grasp anything. Things you can't teach verbally, things it took me fifteen years to be able to do, she had it right away. She just hadn't been given the material. We said in that first year that if you believed in reincarnation she must have danced in a previous life, because once she started studying on a regular basis she went from beginner to advanced in a year. She was driven."

Soon Evelyn was outgrowing her classes so fast that they were forced to change her grading every few weeks. She sponged up learning. For a time the Carters worried that they might be pushing her too hard. But there was no way they could have stopped her. For Evelyn, it was a time of total absorption in dance. When other girls wrote their boyfriends' initials inside hearts, Evelyn wrote "EH loves BP" – Evelyn Hart loves Ballet Practice. It was her secret code.

She hated the days she didn't go to class. To make up for the wasted time, she had her parents install a barre in her bedroom. A plumber was brought in to screw to the wall a three-foot stretch of plumbing pipe, complete with the U-bend that normally goes under the sink; wallpaper was put over the ends so they wouldn't show, a little mirror was installed nearby, and that was her barre. She did her preliminary stretches on the carpet in front of the mirror in her parents' room next door. Her practice costume at home was a T-shirt over tights. Still, nothing she did was good enough to satisfy her. She wept as she worked – *glissade*-sob, *assemblé*-sniff – because she thought she was so awful. But she always wept in time to the music.

Inevitably, Evelyn and Elly began to drift even further apart. Elly had no interest in dance; she wanted Evelyn to go biking with her and explore their new hometown. Evelyn wasn't interested. She didn't want to do anything except dance. She stopped going to CGIT, spent more and more time at her makeshift barre, and became increasingly reluctant to accompany the family on the annual three-week summer trip to the cottage at Lake Sturgeon. At the cottage she'd spend the time sulking, refusing to water-ski because she said it used the wrong muscles for ballet. Once she became so angry she took the family boat out to the middle of the lake in search of privacy and refused to return. John had to swim out to bring her back.

The family activities that had been such an important part of her life were now a bore. If everyone sat around playing a game, Evelyn would usually choose to do something else. One Christmas the family was expected to visit relatives, but Evelyn didn't want to have anything to do with relatives that Christmas, she wanted to stay home and work on her dancing. Eventually they had to drag her, kicking and screaming, into the car.

Soon Evelyn became so temperamental that Elly spent most of her free time with their older sister, Judy, and Evelyn wonders now whether she might have pushed Elly away from her deliberately, as a means to deal with the conflicts within her that derived from being a twin.

Maxine was the one who took Evelyn's behaviour the hardest. It was almost as if she felt she was losing her daughter to the Carters. Evelyn would sit by her window at night and stare out toward London, wishing she were living with the Carters, who were by now like surrogate parents.

John Hart believes it might have been better for Maxine if she and the Carters had been closer, because it would have helped her to understand Evelyn's single-mindedness, but there has never been any closeness between the two households.

During this time Evelyn began to become obsessive about her weight. Since early childhood she had always equated thinness with beauty, but now – she was in Grade 10 – it was a compulsion. She decided that eighty-two pounds would be her ideal weight, and became determined not to pass that figure; if she weighed any more than that before class on Saturday morning, her weekend was ruined. Some days, she would eat just a spoonful of peanut butter for breakfast, so her stomach wouldn't stick out but she would still have calories to burn (it's a habit that endures to this day).

In the spring of 1971, at the end of Evelyn's first year with the Carters – a year into which she had compressed two normal years of training in the Cecchetti technique – she took a Cecchetti examination with Carole Chadwick, from the National Ballet School. Within minutes of the start of the exam – at the point where the students had just performed their *pliés* – Chadwick invited Evelyn to attend the school's summer session.

To the girl with stars in her eyes, it seemed like another chance for the dream to come true. But it was to lead to her cruellest disappointment yet.

At the end of that summer school, Evelyn was offered a place in the National Ballet School for the coming fall session. It was a traumatic moment for the girl – and the trauma was complicated by the fact that neither her parents nor her teachers were sure that she should go. The Carters travelled to Dorchester to explain to Maxine and Terry Hart their concerns about the possible effect of the school's stylistic restraints on Evelyn's expressiveness, and their fears that – because of her struggles to bring herself up to technical par and her lack of confidence in her own abilities – she would not be emotionally ready for the rigours of the school.

There was also the problem of money. Initially, the school offered Evelyn a quarter-scholarship, which was too little assistance. Then the school raised the offer to a half-scholarship, which Terry also felt obliged to turn down on the grounds that they couldn't afford to pay the balance. Evelyn sank into a trough of disappointment. "Then one day I was out on the verandah," she recalls, "and John came running out. 'Evy! Evy!' he shouted. 'It's Belly Elephant on the phone! They're offering a full scholarship! Just hold out a little longer and they'll be paying you to come!'"

It wasn't an auspicious start. Evelyn regarded the full scholarship not as statement of confidence in her talent but as something the school had been pushed into because of her family's poverty. And she felt out of place in the school as soon as she arrived. Everyone else seemed to have been there before, or to have friends in the school. And even though she had had wonderful teachers, she thought she didn't know a step of what she was doing. She felt totally amateurish: she didn't have the right background, and didn't know how to live the life. The fact that she shared a room with a group of students of mixed academic levels didn't help – they considered themselves the school rejects.

In what was to become a lifelong pattern, she began to take out her vexations on her body and avoided eating whenever she could. Once she hid in a closet because she didn't want to eat breakfast. Her obsession with her weight was heightened by the emphasis that was placed on weight in the school itself. The girls would compete to see which of them could tolerate the hottest bath water, because the heat was supposed to shrink the body's fat cells. They were subjected to regular weigh-ins, with everyone's weight posted on a chart, and to the bewildered child who wanted so much to do the right thing, it seemed

Evelyn's first public performance. She is seen at centre in a Carter studio recital presentation of Blue the Dreamer, *at Oakwood Collegiate School, London, Ontario, in the spring of 1972.*

COURTESY MAXINE HART

that the students who earned praise as the best were always the thin ones; inevitably, she equated balletic talent with thinness. While subconsciously she might have been punishing herself for her imagined shortcomings, to her conscious mind it was simply a matter of making herself more thin, conventionally beautiful, and therefore more acceptable. Being thin helped her fit in.

The same sense of inferiority has dogged her career – if she sees a dancer with what she considers a better-shaped body or hips that are more turned out than hers, she retreats into an insecurity that can be traced back to those first uneasy days at the National Ballet School. Nothing in her early experience conditioned her to believe that she had the instrument to be a world-class dancer.

It didn't take long for the collapse to come. Dorothy Carter recalls going to visit Evelyn at the school when she was in Toronto to do some examining that fall. "She flung herself into my arms, crying her eyes out. Her face looked like a skull; the skin on it looked dreadful." They went to a restaurant nearby, but Evelyn refused to eat, protesting that she was fat.

In some anxiety, Carter contacted the teachers at the school. Two days later, Betty Oliphant contacted Evelyn's parents and asked them to arrange for her to get psychiatric attention.

By early December, Evelyn was home. She weighed seventy-six pounds.

Anorexia nervosa is a condition of self-starvation that often afflicts young women – especially dancers. Sometimes it is accompanied by bulimia, the self-enforced vomiting of recently ingested food. Evelyn had developed a severe case of anorexia, and it was this that had led the school to request her removal. Today, the National Ballet School retains consultants to treat anorexia, and will generally allow affected students to remain at the school during treatment, providing they also receive psychiatric care. But at the time Evelyn was at the school, it was believed that the most effective treatment was for the child to return home and then obtain psychiatric treatment. "One of the things about anorexia," says Betty Oliphant, "is that there's an enormous amount of denial [by the sufferer]. Another aspect is the denial from the family. There's a big sexual thing about anorexia too – it's a fear of growing up. And usually anorexics don't have a very warm relationship with their parents." By those definitions, Evelyn's was a classic case.

At Betty Oliphant's recommendation, Terry and Maxine Hart consulted a psychiatrist in London. They saw him a number of times, sometimes with Evelyn present and sometimes not. The brunt of his advice was that Evelyn should no longer put all her eggs in one basket. He drew parallels with his son, who liked hockey. It was good for his boy to like hockey, but if he allowed him the privilege of doing nothing else, that would be the boy's undoing. Singlemindedness was unhealthy, and it was not a parent's privilege to allow it. His advice to Terry and Maxine was to make sure that Evelyn finished her schooling to Grade 12, and to find her another interest. To Maxine, the psychiatrist's word was not to be questioned; it was professional advice. She began to urge her daughter to spread her interests out.

A rift between mother and daughter opened up. Maxine, acting always in what she considered Evelyn's best interests, began to position herself in direct opposition to the girl's most cherished dreams. The more Evelyn tried to intensify her ballet studies, the more Maxine urged diversification. They were in permanent collision, and the deeper Evelyn involved herself in her dancing, the deeper the wounds became.

Dorothy Carter subsequently told Evelyn that the National Ballet School had been planning to phase Evelyn out of ballet altogether, even before her enforced withdrawal, because the staff believed she lacked the emotional fortitude to succeed as a dancer. That was probably the case. Betty Oliphant had at one point called Evelyn into her office and given her a talking-to; on other occasions, Evelyn would be scheduled for coaching and no teacher would show up. They had taken her on for the school because they could see the extent of the changes that had taken place in her in a single year – but she remained totally out of their league. Hers was still predominantly dance of instinct.

At the time, however, Terry and Maxine were under the impression that once they had arranged for Evelyn to consult a psychiatrist she would be allowed to return to the school. Evelyn thought she would be able to continue treatment for her problems with specialists in Toronto, an assumption reinforced by Betty Oliphant's own assurances that "we always take back kids with anorexia."

So at the beginning of the following term early in January, Maxine and Terry sent Evelyn back to Toronto with her trunk. A neighbour on a business trip gave her a ride to the school. When she arrived, she discovered her bed at the Jarvis Street residence had already been assigned to someone else.

The new failure hit Evelyn hard, and back in Dorchester she slipped into a deep depression. For a time she was so battered by the experience she had trouble motivating herself to dance. She temporarily lost interest in the one thing that she held most dear. She thought she had failed.

Throughout the balance of that academic year, the Carters nursed her carefully back to confidence. At first Evelyn hated the work, particularly the Carters' stringent demands that she increase her weight. But gradually her commitment to dancing returned, and soon she was taking more classes than ever.

Meanwhile, Maxine, still acting on the advice of the psychiatrist, had been looking around for things for Evelyn to do that would take her mind off ballet – for ways to stop her putting all her eggs in the same basket. She settled on a job as a lifeguard at the public swimming pool in Dorchester.

Evelyn's sister Judy was already employed there as a senior guard and teacher. Evelyn was given a job as her assistant, keeping her eye on the kids at the outer reaches of the class, or teaching the pre-beginners how to jump into the water (she'd line them up along the side of the pool and pretend they were soldiers, shooting them bang, bang, bang, and they'd all fall into the water in a row) or how to float like a jellyfish.

She was also expected to take part in the day's first class, for senior swimmers. The class lasted close to an hour each morning, in unheated water that stayed at a constant fifty-two degrees. Late each summer afternoon, in ninety degree weather, she could be found sitting shivering in the manse garden, wrapped in a blanket, sipping hot chocolate.

But she persevered. It was her sixty-four-dollars-a-week salary at the pool that was paying for her ballet lessons. Despite all the upheavals, EH still loved BP, better than anything.

What restored her faith in herself was a trip to New York in the summer of 1972. Dorothy and Victoria Carter were there for a teachers' seminar, and they sent Evelyn a ticket to join them. It was Dorothy's theory that, after her long period of emotional recuperation, Evelyn was ready to tackle the challenge of taking class in a professional environment, outside her familiar home territory.

Evelyn was sixteen, and still had not begun menstruation. Maxine, worried that the girl was not maturing physically, had arranged for her to go into hospital for exploratory surgery that week – "but I wasn't going to give up going to go to New York for surgery, I can tell you," says Evelyn. Three days before she was due to go into hospital, her first period came. "Is that not mentally forcing yourself into maturing?" she asks.

She arranged to get three days clear from her summer job, and hurried off to join her teachers. It was the first time she had ever flown. She dressed up for the occasion in three-quarter-length socks, a short skirt, a little bodysuit with anchors on it (bought at K-Mart with her first swim-instructor's paycheque) and a little knitted hat with a pom-pom. She looked like a twelve-year-old. In the photographs she has kept from that period, there is a radiant, innocent excitement about her smile.

By night, Evelyn "ghosted" in the Carters' room at the Waldorf-Astoria; they pulled apart Vickie's bed, Evelyn sleeping on the mattress and Vickie on the springs. By day, she took class (sometimes audition class) at the city's principal studios, including the American Ballet Theatre – with Maria Swoboda, the former Bolshoi Ballet dancer who established a career as a dancer and teacher in the U.S.A. after leaving Russia in 1917 – the Joffrey Ballet, the Harkness Ballet, and with the American teacher and ballet-master Don Farnworth.

Dorothy and Victoria Carter sat at the front of each class as spectators. If they thought she was doing well they would rub their noses; Evelyn was in a state of panic at each class until she saw them perform the secret gesture. She was so frantic to do well that she did every exercise with every group, rather than dancing and then resting while others danced, as is normally the case in class. Farnworth was so concerned about her stamina that at one point he led her to the barre and instructed her to rest.

She was a big success. In Maria Swoboda's class, Evelyn was the only dancer to be given corrections: a rare honour from a teacher who by that time conducted most of the proceedings from a chair. At the Joffrey Ballet they said they would accept her for the company school if she'd get her academic schooling finished first. The Harkness school offered her a scholarship.

The visit to New York brought about precisely the transformation that Dorothy Carter had hoped for. By the time they came home, Evelyn was wearing flowers in her hair and blossoming with new confidence – just like the dancers she'd seen in the New York companies.

With Evelyn's confidence repaired, the Carters went to work on her technique. Obedient to her parents' wishes, Evelyn assiduously applied herself to the completion of Grade 12 at Lord Dorchester Secondary School. But she also increased her ballet class-load. Maxine probably never knew how many classes her daughter was taking – several evenings during the week, and all day Saturday – but still the rift between mother and daughter continued to widen.

Part of the problem, John Hart speculates, lay with Maxine's difficulty in recognizing that her daughter was no longer her baby, but a growing young woman with a life and ambitions of her own. With Judy and Elly, Maxine was still getting back as much emotional support as she gave, but Evelyn, steadfast to her ambitions and consumed by the conviction that she needed to make up for all those lost years, had little emotional strength left over to give her family.

For Maxine this was hard to accept, particularly when she was investing so much care and love in the girl's emotional well-being.

However, Evelyn in due course graduated from high school, and there were hopes that she would go to university or take some further academic or home-economist courses – a family fund had been established years before to pay for it. When Evelyn attended Grant Strate's summer dance school at York University in Toronto in the summer of 1973, Strate made it clear to Maxine that Evelyn would certainly be welcome to join the full-time York dance program.

However, Evelyn and the Carters had other plans. She was seventeen, she had caught up on technique, she had passed all her major ballet exams, she had arrived at a certain emotional equilibrium, and in Dorothy Carter's view it was time for "the little bird to test her wings." So they decided to send her to ballet school in Winnipeg.

The family scholarship fund for Evelyn's education was eventually cashed in, at a loss.

The professional program of the Royal Winnipeg Ballet's school was estab-lished in 1970 by David Moroni, a former principal dancer with the company. It began as a modest affair, overshadowed by the much larger and longer-established National Ballet School in Toronto. At the time that Evelyn was proposed as a candidate for the program, there was no official audition procedure – teachers would recommend their better students to Moroni, and he or a representative would take a look at them when the company passed through on tour. The Carters duly mentioned the name of Evelyn Hart, "but we decided we wouldn't tell them they had a ballerina coming," says Dorothy. "We wanted to shock them."

Betty Oliphant believes that Evelyn's parents agreed to allow the girl to be put forward for Winnipeg because "we were being punished. We were dying to have her back." Punishment or not, the die was cast in favour of Winnipeg. Evelyn initially auditioned for the school by taking a class with the Royal Winnipeg Ballet when it came to perform at the University of Western Ontario's Alumni Hall in London in February 1973. It was her father's birth-day; he drove her in from Dorchester, and they went to the ballet together that evening.

What she did was enough to win her an invitation from ballet master Vernon Lusby to come to the school the following fall. At home, it was a difficult moment. The feeling that she should continue her schooling was strong. But the Carters knew she couldn't wait until she had finished Grade

13, and Evelyn was convinced this was her last hope. So Maxine packed her bags for her and off they went.

The girl had not, in fact, been given a firm invitation to join the school; she had merely been invited to Winnipeg for further auditions. The journey was not yet over.

Evelyn and her mother arrived in Winnipeg on a Saturday in September 1973. The following morning the minister of Winnipeg's Regents Park United Church, Douglas Snell – a former assistant to Terry Hart in his Peterborough ministry – made an appeal from the pulpit for accommodation for "a young lady who needs a place to stay for a few days."

In the congregation was Kay Marchbank. She had the impression that the minister was looking directly at her as he made his appeal. Her son Cambell had been married the previous day and she now had a spare room. She stopped by the church door on the way out, volunteered the space, and that evening Snell brought the girl and her mother round. The understanding was clear; Evelyn just needed short-term accommodation. As she left, Maxine handed Kay an airline ticket and asked her to put Evelyn on a flight to Toronto as soon as the auditions were over.

At the auditions themselves, Evelyn was her usual tentative self, entirely lacking in confidence and certain she was doing all the wrong things – arms all over the place, emoting too much, missing combinations.

For the first three days, she wasn't even aware that she was being taught by Moroni. All she had to go on as an example for procedure was her audition process at the National Ballet School, where the director, Betty Oliphant, sat behind a table throughout. She kept waiting for the principal of the school to turn up. Meanwhile, she says, they were being taught by "this man with a green sweater round his neck – quite good-looking, a kind of warm air about him, beautiful lips and beautiful blue eyes. I thought this was someone quite else – and when after three days I found out it was David Moroni I just about died."

So did Moroni, but for different reasons. "I can remember looking at her and thinking, 'Oh my God, what are we going to do with this kid? She's so wild!'" he once recalled. "We just labelled her 'The Wild One.' I didn't know what her name was but I recognized there was a great individual right then and there. It did scare me. I thought, 'Oh boy, how am I going to handle this?'"

Arnold Spohr, who was artistic director of the company at the time Evelyn auditioned, and who later reshaped the company's repertoire in large part to accommodate her talents, remembers her arrival. "At class, this one girl always

WALTER O. WEBER

David Moroni helps Evelyn in her placement in a Royal Winnipeg Ballet school tour warm-up class, spring, 1975.

caught my eye. Long arms and all legs, very expressive, moved in her own manner, with a tremendous freedom – more than she needed to move with, even then. She definitely had projection, musicality, and a charisma already. The thing I remember too was her joy in what she was doing, a joy from inside. It wasn't just smiling and peripheral, it was movement catching the vitality and energy of dance with the particular aura that was already hers – and that was unusual. It was a rare thing to see. How many students have I seen come in with so much? Feet, legs, coordination, intelligence; everything was there."

However, no immediate decisions were made. The audition process dragged on, with Kay Marchbank's husband Verlin (Lin), an estate planning consultant, making periodic checks with Moroni, and Maxine calling from time to time to find out when Evelyn was coming home. Finally, three weeks after the auditions began, Evelyn was offered a permanent place in the school. And by that time she had settled into the Marchbank household so well that they simply made the arrangement permanent. Evelyn stayed with the family for three years.

The Marchbank household became Evelyn's new domestic circle. This was the first time she had lived away from home, and from her twin sister Elly, for any length of time, and at first she found it hard to adjust. But Lin and Kay Marchbank are decent, straightforward, church-going folk, without a great deal of fussiness about them; from the start, they simply treated Evelyn like another of their children.

It helped enormously that their daughter, Cynthia (Cindy), was just a year younger than Evelyn; she became a replacement figure for Evelyn's lost twin. They hit it off right away. Cindy also provided a valuable outlet for Evelyn from the pressures of the ballet world. She could come home and talk about the terrible day she'd had, the little things that had gone wrong in class, and find a ready listener. Most evenings the girls sat and talked. Lin and Kay Marchbank, holding the view that part of their duties as parents was to listen and advise, would often join them. Since none of the Marchbanks knew the remotest thing about ballet before Evelyn arrived on their doorstep, all three learned a lot.

With Cindy in particular, Evelyn was always ready to demonstrate the latest moves she had learned, putting her music on the record-player and dancing round the living room in her nightgown.

Many times Cindy was cast as the male partner, holding Evelyn while she struck her poses. Lin Marchbank's most vivid recollection from those times is Evelyn's determination. "She'd come home with her feet blistered and bleeding, but she'd have a bath and put on her housecoat and then she'd be in the living room with the music cranked up and she'd say, 'I'm going to do it all night if I have to.'"

Cindy, a typical teenager, was into her school life and socializing with her friends. She often tried to get Evelyn to go out with her, without much success. But they did go walking a lot by the river, strolling in summer to an ice-cream place called the BDI, or, in mid-winter, putting on their old coats and hiking through the frost and snow for miles. "She'll break a leg to make people happy," says Cindy. "At Hallowe'en and things like that she'd always show off. One Christmas she was a reindeer: antlers, great big eyelashes. She went prancing into the rehearsal hall. And I'd always get the pre-showing." "She was a tremendous actor," says Lin. "She'd entertain everybody who came to the house. She loved to sit in a family group and tell stories."

It was by no means all happiness. Despite the best and most loving intentions of the Marchbank family, Evelyn was sometimes terribly lonely. And the work was hard; she'd leave the house early in the morning, and not return until after 6:00 in the evening, physically and emotionally exhausted.

And eating was, as usual, a problem. Early on, Maxine came up with a list of Evelyn's preferences, but Kay told her: "Well, I just make ordinary plain meals, and if she's going to be with us she's going to have to be part of the family." Even so, Kay makes no secret of the fact that the eating habits of their new "daughter" were sometimes a worry. "She didn't really like a plateful of meat," recalls Kay. "She's a snacker," says Lin. "The crackers, the raisins, the peanut butter, and the tea – that's what I remember about her diet. And granola. We decided after a period of time – even though we really believe in a balanced diet – that we shouldn't harass her: we should encourage her lovingly."

Cindy remembers Evelyn as a great help with her own weight problems. "She'd make my lunches for me. But she never sat down and ate many meals with us – she'd get in a little after six and she'd munch on peanut butter. But my mum was paranoid that she's die on us if she didn't eat, so she always kept chicken handy. Evelyn liked chicken. She'll eat; but she's very conscious of her weight."

Evelyn was also a good source of opinion on girl matters, the sort of things a girl couldn't ask her mother about. Cindy was just starting to date, and she'd ask Evelyn's advice. Evelyn didn't have much in the way of experience, but she brought an objective view.

The Marchbanks all have special memories of Evelyn's kindness. Once, toward the end of her stay with the family, Evelyn brought a fellow student home for supper and asked if she could be accommodated for a day or two because she had nowhere else to stay. The girl was someone Evelyn looked on as a rival, but she put her negative feelings aside because she knew she was looking for somewhere to live. "I think this was a hard thing for Evelyn to do," says Lin, "but she was giving enough to know that the girl needed a place to stay."

Cindy and Evelyn remained good friends even when Evelyn had moved away. When Cindy was married, in the fall of 1979, Evelyn made all the bridesmaids' hairpieces. She stayed with Cindy the night before the ceremony, sewing pearls onto her wedding dress, helping with the alterations, the two girls laughing and talking together into the small hours. Though they don't stay in touch any longer as much as Cindy might like, Evelyn still collects matchbooks wherever she travels for Cindy's husband, Julien Cormier; the collection sits in a big glass container on a shelf of their Winnipeg home. Cindy says (as do so many others who regret the way that Evelyn's work and success have taken her from their lives) on the occasions when they do meet, it's as if they have never been apart.

Evelyn's early years at the RWB professional program did not go smoothly. "The Wild One" lived up to her name. "She had that extra freedom that had to be harnessed," says Spohr, "like a thoroughbred ready to go but needing that touch of discipline, refining away that excess that you just didn't need."

WALTER O. WEBER

Evelyn in her second year in the RWB's professional division, fall 1974, with teacher Jacqueline Weber, now division vice-principal.

Perhaps identifying even then qualities of expressiveness in her work that reminded him of the Russian style of dancing he has always so admired, Spohr began to call her "Little Miss Leningrad." At that time, she had never had a day of Russian training in her life.

Responding in her instinctive, visceral way to the music, she sometimes went over the top, and her technique and timing suffered. And everything was always a drama. "Often she would break into tears in the middle of class," Moroni once recalled, "and one day I said to her, 'Lookit, one tear rolls down the face, you have to leave class, dry the tear, then you can come back.'" David Peregrine, who later won medals partnering her in international competition, went to class to see the new girl with "the back made of bubble gum" and was taken aback to see her suddenly burst into tears.

Cathy Taylor, who became assistant to both Spohr and Henny Jurriens as artistic directors and eventually part of the triumvirate that ran the company immediately after Jurriens' death, entered the RWB professional program a matter of months before Evelyn. She had previously studied at the National Ballet School (she knew Evelyn vaguely from those years – "she was there and she was gone"), and had transferred to Winnipeg, as had a number of other National Ballet School students, after it was made clear to her that she was not National Ballet material.

She and Evelyn were initially in the same Moroni class at Winnipeg. "I didn't see her first as anything special: she was another dancer – very nice legs and feet, kind of weak, like a colt." But as the talent began to make itself apparent, the problems began to grow. It was as if, for Moroni, no one else existed in the class.

"We used to say we could do triple pirouettes on our heads and he wouldn't notice us," says Taylor. "It was like tunnel vision. It was discouraging, difficult to survive that. It must have been horrible for her too, but at the time, I was just a dancer, I wanted correction and guidance and wanted to go forward, and all of a sudden you were left alone and you had to cope with it."

That singling-out was inevitable. Despite a recent influx of well-trained students (including Taylor) from the National Ballet School, Moroni had never before been faced with such potential talent. And if it was scary, it was also thrilling.

For Evelyn, Moroni was her escape from southwestern Ontario into the world of professional dance. In those early years, she felt her life was held in debt to him and her future was at his disposal. She placed her self-image and self-esteem in his hands; she trusted him implicitly. Subconsciously, she later realized, she saw him as surrogate father, and then as surrogate lover. "I remember when I first went to the school and I'd go to the ballet and he'd walk into the lobby, and my breath would go, o-o-oh – in one sense terrified, but trembling with excitement. I was in love with the man."

She stayed in the school for three years, building her technique, reinforcing her self-confidence, and beginning to make contact with the classical pas de deux.

She danced with the company often as a student, initially in the outdoor summer shows in Assiniboine Park. Her first main-season appearance with the company was on October 2, 1974, as part of the corps de ballet in Agnes de Mille's *Fall River Legend* – on a program that also included Mikhail Baryshnikov's historic first performance in the West after his defection four months earlier from the Kirov Ballet.

She left for that all-important debut a little disappointed, Kay Marchbank told the Harts, because there was "no word from home. But I know you wish her well. We are always telling the mailman we would like more letters." But the performance itself was a great excitement. "All the New York critics were there," minister Doug Snell, who attended the show, wrote to the Harts. "All kinds of people flew in from N.Y., Toronto, Vancouver, etc., to witness the event. And there was Ev in the middle of it all! And she did very well. It was no run-on bit part either – it was a big part and a good one!"

At the end of her second season, Spohr wanted her full-time for the company, but Moroni, arguing that she wasn't yet psychologically ready for the strain, suggested she stay in the school for an extra year to give her a chance to reach a more balanced personal well-being, and Spohr deferred to the advice.

Her last performance as a member of the school was in the spring of 1976. Her parents travelled to Winnipeg to see the student show; her father, recalls Kay Marchbank, was immensely proud of his daughter. It was the only time he saw her dance; she never had another chance to show him what she called "the product of all my tears." She was on her first tour with the company, the following October, when he died.

Terry Hart took this photograph of his daughter backstage at a performance by the RWB school's professional division in the spring of 1976, just prior to her entry into the company.

DAVID COOPER

David Peregrine and Evelyn share a private moment in the studio, 1979.

3 *The Deer and The Falcon*

*E*velyn Hart entered the Royal Winnipeg Ballet on June 26, 1976, as a member of the corps de ballet. Almost immediately, she found herself in conflict with established dancers who knew her reputation from the school and saw her as a threat. In her first year in John Neumeier's *Nutcracker*, while she was still a member of the corps de ballet, she was cast to do most of the prime non-soloist spots – the pas de quatre, the pas de six. Her talent was clearly exceptional, and her insistence on always looking her best, either on stage or in the practice studio, intensified the challenge to her more established colleagues. "Shouldn't I try to look like a ballerina?" she asked a friend, dancer Gailene Stock, after one particular snubbing. "If you ask me," said Stock, "the rest of them should be doing that too."

None of this rivalry helped Evelyn's self-esteem. From her earliest days at the school, Spohr and Moroni, astute enough to realize that her special talent as an artist was in all likelihood linked to her emotional vulnerability, had understood the importance of providing an environment of care and concentration, a place where the fragile and exceptional flower could be shielded. They also filled another need: they became her friends; people who would always be there for her, people she could trust, people who understood the difficulties and the challenges she was facing.

She made her performance debut as a member of the company at Montreal's Place des Arts in the corps de ballet in Oscar Araiz's *Rite of Spring* – a primitive, leotard-clad interpretation of the Stravinsky music that, in Nijinsky's original 1913 production in Paris by the Diaghilev Ballets Russes, arguably set European modernism on its headlong spiral down the twentieth century.

The Argentinian Araiz, discovered by Spohr during a company trip to Latin America, turned the ballet into a celebration of atavistic bloodforces, set in a prehistoric darkness. He filled it with a feral ferocity, the dancers crawling like insects and fighting like animals. And the girl who had spent her childhood dressing up in the fanciest, laciest offerings in the children's clothing section of her grandfather's store, dreaming of a dancer's life of rhinestones and eye-lashes, found herself out on stage with her hair loose, wearing a little knitted vest, a leotard, and a pair of leg-warmers.

Because of her medium height, she was put into every section of the ballet, including the central "birthing" sequence. "I was the only one who had to do it – the most ugly dance – in a pair of bikini underwear, and me, totally, totally prude and terribly shy. I did it, but I was convinced I was terrible. My hair was so long I'd crawl up onto it and end up with my neck caught, trying to shift myself along, and I thought, oh screw it. To me this was not ballet." (In this view she kept company with the then-president of Argentina, who pro-claimed that Araiz's *Rite* contained "objectionable" erotic overtones. On the other hand, she was at odds with New York's Robert Joffrey, who took one look at the RWB's *Rite* and promptly invited Araiz to New York to mount something for his company.)

Her other big number was in Paddy Stone's pop-dance, *The Hands*, which called mainly for jazz kicks. For the entire first year she never seemed to get to do anything in pointe shoes.

Where were the princess dresses she had dreamed of so ardently? Where was the fairy-tale glamour that ballet was really all about? It was on its way; and more of it than she might have imagined. But she still keeps a letter of resignation she wrote, but never sent, after that first season, to remind herself of what she went through, and to reassure herself that patience and persever-ance does, in the end, pay off.

One of Spohr's long-term ambitions when he took over direction of the company in 1958 was to provide his dancers with the best possible technical training, and he travelled the ballet world for a decade, checking out a variety of schools and styles before settling on the Vaganova technique, on which the pure and unmannered style of Leningrad's Kirov Ballet is based.

As mentor and inspiration he chose Vera Volkova, the former artistic adviser to the Royal Danish Ballet and, until her death in 1975, the leading authority in the West on the theories of Agrippina Vaganova, the Russian teacher who first synthesized a variety of ballet techniques into her own celebrated style. Spohr travelled annually for almost a decade in the late 1960s to watch Volkova at work and was able to persuade her to spend several summers teaching in Winnipeg and at the Banff Centre summer dance session, a teaching facility with which the company had links.

In the late 1970s, Volkova was succeeded as visiting Vaganova pedagogue by a series of Russian teachers, one of the first being Natalia Zolatova, then head of a school outside Moscow. In the summer of 1977, Evelyn was chosen to go to the summer dance session with Zolatova in Banff and be part of the Banff festival company. It was the end of Evelyn's first season with the RWB; she was still a member of the corps de ballet. Company principals Bonnie Wyckoff, Roger Shim, Salvatore Aiello, and Marina Eglevsky had originally been scheduled to study with Zolatova and dance the leads in *Les Sylphides* and *The Sleeping Beauty* pas de deux, but Wyckoff was unable to make the trip and Spohr selected Evelyn to take her place.

This was not Evelyn's first visit to the popular and well-established summer school. The previous year she and David Peregrine had impressed Cuban choreographer Jorge Garcia (there to set *Paquita* on the Banff festival company) with their performance of the pas de deux from *Nutcracker*, which they had learned at school in Winnipeg. Garcia became an early Hart fan, and subsequently recommended her for guest engagements in a number of companies.

In 1977 it was Zolatova's turn to be impressed. Evelyn danced the pas de deux from *The Sleeping Beauty* with Shim, and Zolatova – a tiny, compact woman in her mid-forties, with twinkling, dark-brown eyes – suggested privately to Spohr at the end of the summer session that he consider sending Evelyn to the international ballet competition at Varna, Bulgaria – a contest generally regarded as the world's most important.

Spohr did not act on that recommendation at the time. But Zolatova's enthusiasm for the young dancer gave him the confidence to cast Evelyn in the principal role of Louise, in Neumeier's *Nutcracker*, the following fall. Louise was a role that marked the beginning of Evelyn's public recognition. For the first time, people outside the company began to sit up and take interest – though when Evelyn's mother travelled to Winnipeg to see her in the role, she didn't recognize her. Evelyn told her she was the dancer in green, and after the show Maxine said, "Well, there were two in green, which one were you?"

Until that time, Evelyn had always felt too shy to attend the parties that were thrown for the company on tour. But that week she went to her first reception,

DAVID COOPER

Evelyn with David Peregrine in Les Sylphides, *a role she first learned in 1977.*

hosted by a member of the Vancouver Ballet Society. She wore the most expensive dress she had ever bought – an eighty-dollar number by Monique Gabin, grey, knitted, sleeveless, with burgundy and gold silk thread woven into the low-cut top, and a burgundy turtleneck beneath. "Very nice," said Vancouver impresario David Y. H. Lui, who regularly presented the company's Vancouver visits. "But, darling, where are your rings? If you're going to be a star we have to get someone to buy you rings." That was the beginning of a close and enduring friendship.

Although by now she had full access to company teaching, Evelyn supplemented her training by continuing classes with Moroni's professional program. And in 1977 she moved out of the Marchbank home and into a shared apartment at The Bessborough, a downtown apartment block, with one of Moroni's students, Julie Wilson. They lived together for two years, then Wilson was succeeded by another student from London, Suzanne Jaeger. Shortly thereafter, the ménage became a trio, when a student from Vancouver, Sarah Slipper, also moved in.

Slipper, later to become a soloist with the company, was five years younger than Evelyn and somewhat in awe of her. They met on the street one cold day in the fall, started to chat, and eventually went to a movie together – *Heaven Can Wait*, with Warren Beatty. To this day it is one of their favourite films. "Then we went out for coffee," says Slipper, "and we talked and talked and talked, two little ballet bunheads, and that's how our friendship grew. Not long after that I lost a roommate and didn't know where to go, and it all worked out." Suzanne Jaeger moved out soon after, and Evelyn and Sarah Slipper spent the next three years together.

Inevitably, they influenced each other. Evelyn taught Sarah about dedication to dance and about the life of ballet. Sarah taught Evelyn about life outside the ballet studio, weaning her away from parsimonious practices such as using the same tea-bag cup after cup, showing her it was okay to buy furniture and a brass bed at auction rather than live on boxes and sleep on a mattress on the floor, and helping her develop a sense of style in her dress and her surroundings.

At the same time, Evelyn's natural generosity often pushed to the surface. Since she was the one with the income, she actually paid for most of the furniture, and until Slipper became a member of the company Evelyn always paid for more than her half of shared expenses because she felt she was the earning half of the partnership.

Their dedication to their art drew them together. Sarah was as neurotically wedded to dancing as Evelyn; both worked extra hours at the studio and had very little in the way of hobbies or social life. To relax, they pored over dance books, listened to classical music, went for weekend walks together, and talked incessantly over pots of tea.

Eventually Slipper established a long-term relationship with André Lewis, but when she and Evelyn shared their apartment men were never part of the picture. "We'd talk about our perfect man. He had to be tall, not necessarily a dancer, but well-off, but then, you know, you knew it wouldn't fit. I think Evy still lives with that a bit. It wouldn't fit in your life, it would disturb you."

Anorexia was never far from their thoughts or their lives in those years. It is a common problem in dance. Anorexia is such a threat to dancers that the RWB (like other companies) regularly arranges for nutritionists and medical experts to advise the company members on proper eating habits. The problem is that extra weight is immediately evident on stage. Taken to extremes, it can obviously make dancing (particularly partnering) more difficult. And while the experts may say it's fine for one dancer to be full-breasted or another to have fuller hips, that doesn't carry over to the stage; even an average body isn't that attractive in leotard and tights. So the choice often comes down to being average or being a dancer.

Slipper had already experienced the condition before she and Evelyn moved in together. At one point, she had been asked to leave the school until she had it under control. The problem with anorexia, says Slipper, is that "it's like alcoholism. You probably deal with it for the rest of your life. I've slipped back since then, but I know that was one of my worst periods. She saw me through those young years."

In Slipper's view, though, their anorexia came from different sources. "Evelyn always had this image that the thinner you were, the better you were. With me it was paranoia about my height."

Evelyn does have a compulsion to stay thin. Her mother, Maxine, wonders whether the diet regime she undertook before the birth of Evelyn and her twin sister Elly had anything to do with her subsequent eating disorders. From Evelyn's earliest years, thinness was equated in her mind with acceptability as a dancer (Elly recalls that "whenever she saw breasts developing, she'd cut back [on food]") so if she couldn't make the grade in terms of technique, at least she could demonstrate that she had the right body. As well, whenever Evelyn has been in a difficult situation, or tormented by self-doubt, eating was the first thing to go. Some people drink to escape, some people take drugs; but if Evelyn felt she had given a terrible performance, or failed to respond to a challenge in a satisfactory way, she punished her body by not eating. She has this tendency to punish herself more under control now, though it is never far from the surface. "It never leaves you," she has said. "You rely on your friends for help."

But life for Evelyn and Sarah Slipper was by no means all anorexia and anxiety. They laughed together, they spent Christmas together, singing carols at the top of their voices beside the tree in their apartment. It was as if Evelyn had found a substitute sister. Slipper remembers a real bond of caring between them. "You'd be upset about, say, not getting a part, and she'd put her arm round you and you'd be in tears, all miserable, and she'd have her skinny little arm round you. Hugging her is like there's nothing there; when I hug her I feel like the Jolly Green Giant."

They made ideal sounding-boards for each other – the young student just finding her way into dance, and the young professional already being groomed for stardom.

It was a subtle grooming, but consistent. After *Nutcracker* Evelyn went back into the corps, but in the summer of 1978 she was promoted to soloist. That year, Moroni brought in another Russian teacher, Ludmilla Bogomolova, for the professional program's summer school. Dancer and teacher got on well.

Now the company began to give serious thought to the question of who Evelyn's permanent partner might be. Roger Shim, who had partnered her in the 1977 fall *Nutcracker* performances, was a valiant worker and cut an attractive dash, but ultimately he didn't measure up to her potential. The choice instead came down to Welsh-born, Ottawa-raised David Peregrine, a fellow product of Moroni's professional program, a former partner from the school, and one of the few dancers in the company with the technical facility to match hers.

The partnership began on a note of great promise. Peregrine was a year older than Evelyn, already rising in the company, and in her eyes it was a matter of prestige to be his partner. "I adored him," she says. "He was the big guy, the big league." Evelyn recalls some of the "merit" gifts (traditional exchanges between dancers in the RWB) that he gave her in those early years: a pair of

Visiting teacher Ludmilla Bogomolova (right) demonstrates as Evelyn looks on during the 1979 summer school at Tache Hall, University of Manitoba.

WALTER O. WEBER

gold earrings with green and blue stones after a guest appearance together in
Grand Forks; a book about Karen Kain and Frank Augustyn after performing
Nutcracker in Calgary, Edmonton, Vancouver, and Seattle that season. They
were both interested in making the partnership work.

By early 1979, the proposal to send Evelyn to Varna was being seriously
discussed at the top levels of RWB management – but not with Evelyn. When
an interviewer, tipped off from inside the company, mentioned it casually to
Evelyn during a live television appearance, she was speechless; no one had
mentioned a thing about it to her.

But by mid-1979 the proposal was out in the open. The company had come
through a major upheaval the previous spring; Spohr's leadership had been
unsuccessfully challenged and a number of senior staff and dancers had left.
Evelyn was about to be promoted to principal status, alongside Bonnie
Wyckoff, who was returning after a year as guest with the Joffrey Ballet in New
York.

Spohr had written to Evelyn that February: "Keep your spirits up and don't
let the self-centred, selfish world get you down. Think of the good future and
positive life you will have. God shall give you *good health* so that you can fulfil
your purpose on this earth. It is up to David and myself to make it right for you
and *we will*! You are here for this reason – to bring joy, beauty, love, magic, and
your *mark* in this artistic lifetime. You will leave inspiration that will be
remembered in the time to come."

Varna was to be the start of it. An international showcase was something her
talent demanded; she was the company's first real classical ballerina.

The idea was given vivid reinforcement by Bogomolova that summer, when
she returned to teach at the summer school. She taught Evelyn the pas de
deux from *Giselle* and *Don Quixote*, and when she saw her do the *Giselle* run-
through with André Lewis (then still a student at the school) she leaned over
to Moroni and said: "That girl doesn't dance Giselle. She *is* Giselle."

Strengthened by this enthusiasm from outside the company, Spohr and
Moroni (who had been promoted, after the springtime upheavals, to the post
of associate artistic director, with control of day-to-day activities) decided she
should be entered in the 1980 Varna competition, with Peregrine travelling as
her non-competing partner.

While they agreed that Varna would be valuable experience for her as a
developing artist, Spohr and Moroni privately entertained no real hopes of
success. Evelyn, however, immediately set her sights on the crown. While she
recognized that the best way to protect herself emotionally and professionally
would be to treat the competition simply as experience, her competitive
nature insisted she do her best. She didn't *expect* to win, and didn't think she

Evelyn and André Lewis, her first Albrecht, rehearse Giselle *for the 1979 summer school performance at the University of Manitoba.*

WALTER O. WEBER

had the slightest chance. But she certainly wanted to. She wanted the grand prize. Evelyn Hart wanted it all.

Evelyn remembers the 1979-1980 season as a "golden year." It was the year she was promoted to principal dancer, and it was the beginning of what Spohr called his Dutch connection – the importation of a leading wave of choreographers from Holland, the newly-influential school of creators in Europe who blended classicism and modernism in a direct and unsentimental manner. In the summer of 1979 Spohr sent me a typically breathless and enthusiastic postcard from Amsterdam: "The choreographic talent in Holland is *unbelievable*," he said. "We are moving to a HEALTHY brilliant future extended by the fantastic talent of Hans van Manen, Rudi van Dantzig, and Jiří Kylián. The latter is a *genius*! This is our Dutch period."

   Jiří Kylián would enter Evelyn's professional life in a significant way at a later date, remaking for her a ballet that would become one of her great signature-pieces around the world, the *Nuages* pas de deux. But the 1979-80 season was the year she made contact with Hans van Manen's lyric-expressive *Songs Without Words*; it was also the year Rudi van Dantzig visited the company and picked her out to dance in the RWB première of his atmospheric and moving discourse on separation and death, *Four Last Songs*.

DAVID LANDY

Evelyn Hart with RWB colleague Joost Pelt in Hans van Manen's Songs Without Words, *1979-80 season.*

Van Manen found her so much better than the dancer his assistant had originally cast in the lead for *Songs Without Words* that he took the almost unprecedented step of replacing the original dancer with Evelyn. (However, when the company acquired van Manen's *Five Tangos* the following summer, Evelyn, who had from the start gravitated to van Manen's energy and style, was piqued and mortified to be given only second-cast ranking for a role she had hoped would be hers, with first-cast placement going to a soloist, Kathleen Duffy. The reason, she discovered, was that van Manen's assistant, who mounted the ballet, had thought her too flowery and too "Russian" to be able to deliver to full effect the harsh, somewhat angular style that van Manen uses in this work. Undaunted, Evelyn booked herself some studio time, recruited a regisseur as private coach, worked assiduously for two weeks on mastering the van Manen manner, and won the role back.)

Van Dantzig's first encounter with Evelyn occurred when he arrived to set *Four Last Songs*. "They were doing class. There was a balcony to Arnold's office, and I looked down at the class, because I wanted to see her, this girl I had been told about. And it was so easy to pick her out. I thought, *aha!* In those few seconds, I could see that she moved in a very refined way, very delicate and yet still very strong. That was just a glimpse. Then later in rehearsals, looking close up, I saw a bit more, and then when I rehearsed I became really aware of her determination, her strength, and her incredible gift. It's sometimes amazing that nature gives a body and a mind, everything together, to one person – the musicality, the drive, everything."

He was so impressed with Evelyn he gave her a gift of his pas de deux, *Moments Shared*. Originally choreographed for a married couple in his own Dutch National Ballet as their last performance before retiring, the romantic, lyrical work, set to piano music by Chopin, tells of intimacies between a man and a woman. Van Dantzig took time after rehearsals to teach the piece to Evelyn and David Peregrine, and it remains in the company repertoire. Typically, Evelyn subsequently made adjustments to the choreography to fit it to her own expressiveness, and when she travelled much later to Amsterdam as a guest artist with the Dutch National Ballet and danced it for van Dantzig, he teasingly told her: "I couldn't have done it better myself."

The 1979-80 season was also the time when she and Peregrine began to work on Norbert Vesak's *Belong*, a work that would play a pivotal role in their joint future, bringing them international contest medals and providing them with an instantly accessible, internationally acclaimed visiting-card.

Belong is a pas de deux from *What to do Till the Messiah Comes*, Canadian choreographer Vesak's second work for the RWB, made in 1973. The title for the work was taken from a touch-therapy book of the same name by Bernard Gunther, and in Vesak's words the theme was the belief that, "till the Messiah comes, man should try to make the world a better and a happier place in which to live." With its fashionable sensitivity-awareness theme, its modern-istic use of the body, and its techno-cross music (a mix of material from the rock groups Chilliwack and Syrinx and electronic-music experimenter Phillip Werren), the original work became one of the company's most popular ballets, both at home and on tour internationally.

Belong was extracted from the full-length work in the late 1970s. The RWB has always maintained a stock of pas de deux to give variety to its programs of mixed repertoire, and Spohr was always keen to balance the classical seg-ments, such as the *Don Quixote*, *Le Corsaire*, and *Nutcracker* pas de deux, with duets in a more contemporary vein, such as Michael Smuin's *Eternal Idol*, Oscar Araiz's *Adagietto*, and Rudi van Dantzig's *Moments Shared*.

In style, the look of *Belong* is what once would have been called *adagio plastique* – a yearning, romantic athleticism. It begins with the couple, clad in pale blue bodysuits, stretching and embracing on the floor in a pool of light, and progresses through a series of passionate couplings and partings to an ecstatic, high-borne conclusion of dramatic lifts. There is a sensational, spectacular element to the work: at one point, the woman leaps into a full-split sitting position, supported on the man's outstretched arms at the level of his shoulders. *The Globe and Mail* reviewer Alina Gildiner once wrote that "it's so extraordinary that, while it makes you think of things sublime, it also makes you wish for things irreverent. If this is what Hart, Peregrine, and Vesak will be doing till the Messiah comes, then I can only hope He takes his time."

"It is an adagio act pretending to be art," veteran English critic Clement Crisp once wrote, "with a score of whining echo-chambered awfulness, but the curling and unfurling of two beautiful bodies commands our unstinted admiration, and the dancers persuade us that it is really art pretending to be an adagio act."

Asked about the work's appeal in an interview that accompanies the film of *Belong* made in 1980 by CKND-TV in Winnipeg, Evelyn said, "Perhaps it's to do with its total feeling of tenderness, the intimate feeling, the contact – though not in an exceptionally vulgar way. I don't feel particularly erotic when we're performing the pas de deux – I feel more gentle and more spiritual."

In the early days of their pairing, Evelyn and David Peregrine enjoyed dancing together. "We felt we had something special, a partnership," she says. Talking about dancing *Belong* in that same television interview, Peregrine said, "There are moments when I don't do anything but look at Evelyn, and sometimes, if it has gone very well, just to look at her gives me a spark." She enjoyed working with him in *Nutcracker*, and was fond of him as a good friend. "I never thought of him in any other way," she says. "In other circumstances, I might possibly have fallen in love with him because of our work together, but he was with Susan [Bennet, another company member] so he was my partner and that was it."

But after the preparations for Varna had been underway for some months, Peregrine decided he didn't simply want to put in all that work just to dance as Evelyn's prop; he wanted to compete as well. Evelyn wasn't altogether happy with that. Peregrine had a tendency to be erratic in his work, brilliant one day, less so the next. And they were already growing apart in their attitudes to their work. Evelyn was a perfectionist, ready to repeat something endlessly until she had it right, and right to her own satisfaction; time and convenience didn't matter. Peregrine saw dance more as a job, less as an all-consuming vocation. Their attitudes were diametrically opposed, and it was inevitable that they would begin to clash.

The first time Evelyn was upset with Peregrine over these differences was during a tour in the pre-Varna season. In Fredericton they clashed over an extra rehearsal; Peregrine refused to attend unless he was paid overtime, and he became angry with Evelyn for refusing to file for overtime as well, "because it would make him look Scroogey," she says.

In Charlottetown, he turned up for a pre-Varna rehearsal with Spohr without having done the warm-up that the body needs for it to work safely. Evelyn
maintains, "he hadn't taken any responsibility to prepare himself for a work
which he knew was for Varna, which he knew he was going to compete in."

The reviews from that tour also suggest that she was beginning to outper-
form him in artistry. When they danced the *Don Quixote* pas de deux in
Georgia in February 1980, the *Atlanta Constitution*'s critic wrote: "Hart was
enchanting . . . Peregrine was a little too cautious, holding back the snap and
crackle of the fire that is the heart of this showy piece." Three weeks later,
when they did the same pas de deux in Ottawa, *The Citizen*'s critic Sandra
Rubin was not impressed by either of them. Hart, she said, is "a light, creamy
dancer, and her interpretation of the celebrated work – although technically
correct – lacked the fire and sharpness needed to make it exciting. As for her
partner, David Peregrine, he was completely out of his depth, and he looked
like he knew it. His partnering was secure, but his solo work was heavy and
earthbound."

Comments on Evelyn's remarkable ability to interpret music through her
body – her musicality – were now commonplace both inside and outside the
company, and considerable care had been taken to match her to a suitable
accompanist. The choice was Earl Stafford, from Thunder Bay, who had
joined the RWB as a rehearsal pianist at about the same time as Evelyn entered
the company. It was Spohr who had the idea of putting them together,
allowing them to play off each other. Both were perfectionists; both were
individualists. Stafford resisted many of the age-encrusted idiosyncrasies of
approach to music for ballet, preferring to search for his own ideal. Evelyn had
from the earliest days been developing her own ideas about ballet playing and
her own particular form of expressiveness. But between the three of them –
Evelyn setting out what she wanted, Stafford responding, Spohr acting as
mediator – they would come up with a common goal and a common interpretation that satisfied them all.

But on the dancing front, Evelyn – increasingly aware of the looming
approach of her big international test – felt beleaguered and alone, responsible not only for herself but for Peregrine as well.

Quite late in the preparations for Varna, it was decided that they would also
enter the World Ballet Concours at Osaka, Japan, which was to take place in
late May and early June. Unlike the Varna contest for individuals, Osaka is a
competition for couples. It is less significant than Varna or Moscow, but Spohr
and Moroni thought it valuable preparation for the big event in Bulgaria in July.

By the time it was decided that Evelyn and Peregrine should enter, the official deadline for applications was past. However, Spohr had met the contest's organizer, Madam Ohya, at the Moscow competition in 1977. In his generous, impetuous way Spohr had scoured the Soviet capital to find flowers to give her when they parted, and they had become friends. So he telephoned her at 4:30 one morning in February 1980, while the company was on tour in Halifax, introduced himself as "the fellow she met in Moscow," apologized for missing the deadline, and asked for permission to enter Hart and Peregrine. A week later the necessary documentation arrived in Winnipeg. A week after that, they were officially entered.

In terms of pieces to dance, they were massively underequipped. The company has always made its livelihood as a compact, portable touring troupe, and at that time the cumbersome full-length classics simply didn't figure in the repertoire. However, the company did have a handful of classical showpiece pas de deux that were used as audience-pleasing *bons-bons* on mixed bills – a version of the *Don Quixote* pas de deux, *de rigueur* for all self-respecting concours participants; a *Nutcracker* pas de deux (not from the familiar Ivanov favourite, but from John Neumeier's revisionist version mounted for the RWB) and the recently-premièred *Belong* pas de deux. That was a start.

Giselle also seemed logical. Everyone said Evelyn was a natural for the role, and she wanted desperately to dance it. But all she knew was the bit she had learned from Bogomolova in summer school, and she had never danced it with Peregrine.

The problems were compounded by the disappearance of her support team in the final weeks of preparation for the competition. Spohr fell sick and was unable to help with the coaching (he was so sick he was unable to accompany the dancers either to Osaka or to Varna). Moroni was called out in Spohr's place to oversee a tour of Quebec.

In tears, Evelyn went to general manager Bill Riske, pleading for help both for herself and for Peregrine. In particular, she said, she needed help with *Giselle*. Riske turned for help to the National Ballet of Canada, and Frank Augustyn, who had shared the award for best couple with Karen Kain at the Moscow competition in 1973, was brought in to coach Evelyn and Peregrine in the role.

It was then that Evelyn's relationship with Moroni began to show the first signs of deterioration. Despite her full understanding of the circumstances, in an obscure way she felt betrayed. The man who had been such a power in her development and such a source of reassurance and encouragement was suddenly not around when she needed him most. She also fell head over heels in love with Augustyn, perhaps out of simple perversity. "I remember consciously thinking to myself that I would let myself fall a little bit for Frank, just because I couldn't live my life just waiting for David Moroni when he's not even there."

She told Moroni about her infatuation with Augustyn when he returned to Winnipeg to help them out in the final few days before they were to fly to Osaka, and he was, she recalls, "terribly jealous." She recognizes that she was, at the same time, tense and demanding and under heavy stress. On the flight to Osaka, she and Moroni reached a reconciliation, but after that their relationship was never the same.

The ten-day Osaka trip in late May and early June was a terrifying experience. The four of them – Evelyn, Peregrine, Moroni, Stafford – were totally intimidated by the arrogant posturing of the French and Russian dancers who travelled with them on the flight from Tokyo to Osaka. And when they arrived in Osaka, the Japanese organizers provided no space for class, gave them minimal time for rehearsal, and shuttled them backward and forward between three different theatres.

Moroni put a brave face on it, giving them barre exercises and some last-minute coaching, but the whole contingent was badly upset and nervous. Evelyn, unable to sleep and shaking constantly, found her differences with Peregrine intensifying. Her method of dealing with her nervousness had always been to throw herself even more vigorously into rehearsal; Peregrine's response was the opposite – he preferred to walk away from it. Strained by the tension of their first experience of performing outside North America, terrorized by the atmosphere of competition, they grew further and further apart.

At that time, the Osaka contest was in its third year. It took place in three rounds. In the first, all entrants (in 1980 there were forty-five couples, from twenty-two countries) danced a classical pas de deux from a specified list of ten. Evelyn and Peregrine did their *Giselle* – the first time they had ever danced it in public.

After the initial judging, on May 28, the remaining pairs – the Winnipeggers included – were each required to perform the *Don Quixote* pas de deux. A second judging on May 30 reduced the list of contenders still further, and these survivors were asked to perform a modern pas de deux and another classical pas de deux not included in the first-round list. Evelyn and Peregrine offered Vesak's *Belong* and John Neumeier's *Nutcracker* pas de deux.

For Evelyn, it was all terror. It was the first time in her dancing career that instead of relaxing after the first few bars of music, she became more tense.

Evelyn and David Peregrine perform the Don Quixote *pas de deux in competition at Osaka, 1980.*

Each time she came off she didn't want to go back on-stage. Nevertheless, their performance was enough to win them third-place bronze medals and a prize of 600,000 yen (at that time, worth about $3,300 Canadian) which they split. The gold medals went to Galina Mezentseva and Vladimir Petrunin of the Soviet Union, and silver medals were won by a Hungarian couple. Vesak took a gold medal for his choreography. Earl Stafford was given honourable mention for his accompaniment.

They came home in triumph to champagne and flowers from a group of about fifty well-wishers at the Winnipeg airport. But under the euphoria, everyone involved was exhausted and demoralized by the experience. Varna, they decided, was off.

4 *"Best Young Dancer in the World"*

She mortgaged everything on an improbable dream.
She gambled and won. She became the fantasy.

– David Peregrine

*T*he Varna International Ballet Competition, initiated at the Bulgarian seaside resort in 1964, was the first and remains the most prestigious of all the international contests (others are held in Moscow, Osaka, and Havana). Held annually until 1966, it has since occurred biennially, with an international jury judging entrants in two classes, junior and senior. It was at Varna that many of today's most prominent international ballet stars first came to international attention, among them Vladimir Vasiliev, Natalia Makarova, Mikhail Baryshnikov, and Galina Panova. While Eastern European entrants have clear advantages, in terms of sponsorship, support, and jury composition, participation in the contest is regarded as significant exposure, and promising dancers from around the world are sent to compete. After the strains of Osaka, it did not seem at first as if Evelyn Hart would be one of them. Her planned Varna participation was the goal toward which she had been striving all season. But she had returned from Japan exhausted and she was by no means sure she wanted to repeat the experience.

No one pushed her. Those who worked closely with her were already learning that it was easier to wait for Evelyn to change her mind than to risk forcing her into an entrenched position by argument. Under the circumstances, Moroni agreed, it was probably best if plans for Varna were abandoned.

With the pressure off, everyone began to relax, and life began to return to normal. And with the pressure off, Evelyn's desire to compete at the top levels

Evelyn and David Peregrine on-stage in their pas de deux from John Neumeier's
Nutcracker *in the final round of the Varna competition, 1980.*

revived. Suddenly her energy returned, her ambition came back into play, and she decided that they should go to Varna after all. Far from deterring her, the trials of Osaka had given her unexpected new strength to face the challenges of Bulgaria.

Spohr was still too ill to travel, so the task of accompanying the team again fell to Moroni. The RWB foursome arrived in the hilly coastal city on the Black Sea on June 29, after a long and arduous trip. Again, circumstances seemed to be conspiring against them. When they arrived at the Black Sea Hotel (where all the competitors were housed) they found no single rooms were available. Rather than have to share with foreign competitors, Evelyn and Peregrine agreed that for one or two nights, until their rooms could be sorted out, they would room together – an arrangement that was officially illegal under the contest rules. Both were tense and nervous, and the tension showed in their attitudes to each other – they even managed to quarrel over something as simple as who would pay for the cost of a rental car to go sightseeing.

The Winnipeggers had been assigned rehearsal space in the basement studio of a church, but on their first day Evelyn and Peregrine opted to give Moroni a breather and attend a class provided by the contest organizers. In charge of the class was Galina Yordanova, a Bulgarian teacher and regisseur. For Evelyn, this accidental encounter was a turning point. Later she was to say that the important thing about Varna was not the medals or the acclaim; what Varna really did for her was introduce her to Yordanova. "This little woman with these shiny eyes gave the heaviest class I'd ever done in my life," says Evelyn. "I was exhausted. But immediately she was giving me all these style details, and I remember thinking that I didn't care if I won or not because the best experience was meeting Galina. That was the beginning. I loved her from the start." The meeting was to have long-term effects on the development of the Royal Winnipeg Ballet – and on Evelyn's career.

That afternoon, all seventy-five pairs of competitors and their coaches attended the ceremonial drawing of lots for first-round performance position, and Evelyn was delighted to spot in the Russian contingent Ludmilla Bogomolova – the one who had first suggested to Spohr that Evelyn go to Varna, and who had also taught Evelyn her first versions of *Giselle* and *Don Quixote*. It was an effusive reunion. For a time, until she was warned off by members of her own team, Bogomolova gave Evelyn and Peregrine impromptu coaching.

The contest ran for sixteen days, with the first round lasting a week. Evelyn and Peregrine danced their *Giselle* early in the proceedings (it was only their second public performance of the pas de deux, and Evelyn's tutu "wasn't even the proper one," says Spohr, "because we hadn't done *Giselle* yet as a full

*With
the traditional
dancers'
good-luck message
scrawled on
her mirror,
Evelyn prepares
to compete at
Varna.*

production, so we hadn't got into that type of tutu"). Then they had to wait through five days of competition to find out whether they were still in the running. There was no official word, but there was plenty of talk. Moroni claims that Evelyn was "immediately pronounced one of the top five Giselles in the world by all the judges and critics." Evelyn herself recalls, "Right from the beginning of the competition people were apparently talking about this girl from Canada. It was pretty exciting. It gave me the feeling that, gosh, maybe I've got a chance."

Clearly, she had. On the Friday of the first week, the competitor list was cut by half. Evelyn and Peregrine were among the survivors. The second round lasted for their entire second week in Varna. The RWB couple danced Rudi van Dantzig's *Moments Shared* and the *Don Quixote* pas de deux, and by the end of the week it was clear they were audience favourites.

The final round of performances began the following Sunday and ran for three nights. Their first contribution was the pas de deux from John Neumeier's *Nutcracker*, followed by Vesak's *Belong*. The international rivalry was intense. When it became clear that the Canadians were heading for the winning spot, one of the Soviet members of the jury, Sophia Golovkina, a former Bolshoi Ballet star and subsequent director of the Bolshoi school, tried to have Hart and Peregrine disqualified on the grounds that Neumeier's individualistic and technically challenging variant on *Nutcracker* was not the standard version. But fellow jury member Robert Joffrey objected, pointing out that the Neumeier version had been accepted when the dancers were first entered for the contest,

NICK A. SARABANOS

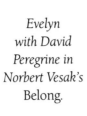

*Evelyn
with David
Peregrine in
Norbert Vesak's*
Belong.

and arguing that it would be unfair to renege on that acceptance now. Golovkina also attempted unsuccessfully to have Evelyn disqualified on the grounds that she didn't complete thirty-two *fouettés* in her solo variation.

Right to the final moments of the contest, there was doubt whether Evelyn would be awarded the top prize, although even before the results were announced she had received invitations to dance in ten cities, among them Paris, New Orleans, Munich, Helsinki, Tokyo, and Sofia. From the first round, her score had consistently placed her ahead of the Soviet Union's Alla Khamaschvili, who had been widely expected to take the top prize. And as the contest climax approached, there was some discussion of the possibility of awarding *two* gold medals, or, alternatively, not awarding a gold medal at all, rather than having to give it to a non-Soviet entrant.

Their performance of *Belong* sealed the Canadians' success, although they had only given it a single on-stage rehearsal, at midnight (all rehearsals were open, and Moroni was afraid that the Russians, who attended everyone's rehearsals, would steal the choreographic material for themselves). After more than a fortnight of posture-perfect pas de deux from the classics, Vesak's lyrical modernism must have wafted over the jurors, the critics, and the balletomane audience like a summer breeze. It literally stopped the show.

The videotape made by Bulgarian state television repeatedly cuts away from the dancers to the audience, which breaks into rapturous applause and calls the dancers back again and again for curtain-calls. Off-stage, they are greeted and congratulated by Moroni and Stafford, both of whom give Evelyn a kiss, and then they run back out for more applause.

The videotape shows just ten curtain-calls. Some people who were there say there were between twenty and thirty, although Evelyn says they stopped counting after fourteen. Moroni said later that the curtain-calls were eventually stopped on the orders of the competition secretariat.

Even then, the final outcome was still technically in question, since two couples, one from the U.S.A. and one from the Soviet Union, still had to dance, though no one by then really had much doubt about the way the decision would fall.

Actual scores were never revealed. But despite Evelyn's conviction that what she and Peregrine did in Varna was not as good as what they could do on a stage at home, she gained more points in the contest than anyone since Vladimir Vasiliev in the contest's debut in 1964. The spread between Evelyn and Khamaschvili was so great that it was impossible for the prize not to be awarded. Along with her gold medal (the only gold won by a Western woman to that time in the competition's history) Evelyn also won the year's only Exceptional Achievement Award. Khamaschvili also gave her, as a friendly memento of their rivalry, a brass plate, which she treasures. Peregrine, who took one of three bronze medals awarded, was the only non-Soviet male dancer in the medal standings. As well, Vesak took the gold medal for his choreography of *Belong*, and Earl Stafford was given a gold achievement award (shared with a Soviet pianist) for the best accompanist in the competition. (Ironically, this was the one RWB award in which *Belong* had no part to play; Vesak's work is performed to taped music. Stafford's achievement was based on his playing for the dancers' four other pas de deux. The woman who shared first place with him, on the other hand, played for all the Soviet entries, and was heard about a hundred times.)

Communications between Bulgaria and the outside world were so bad that Winnipeg didn't hear a word until the contest ended. While they waited the RWB company expected the worst. The news finally came in a roundabout way, via a telephone call from Peregrine to his girlfriend, Susan Bennet. She told the rest of the company and called his mother in Ottawa. His mother telephoned the newspapers, and the tale of the success spread from there.

When the news finally came through, Spohr and his colleagues were flabbergasted. Although he and Moroni had begun to realize something was up after the successes in Japan, not even in their wildest dreams would they have predicted medals at Varna. "What a thrilling, happy day it is!" he wrote, in a circular letter to his friends throughout the ballet world. "I am, to put it mildly, ecstatic. This is the beginning and proof of our professional program, our Canadian identity with David Moroni and all the others. This is only the beginning of another fantastic era for the Royal Winnipeg Ballet." And in a scribbled note on the bottom of some of the letters, he wrote: "Harmony brings the BEST results."

Moroni, who had broken down in tears of joy and relief backstage after the announcement, was always resentful of the way in which the success was underplayed by the media in Canada. He felt that no one in Canada really appreciated what had been achieved. However, the contingent finally reached home to another enthusiastic airport welcome, and congratulatory telegrams for all from the Canada Council and Prime Minister Pierre Trudeau. Vesak, who had relocated to the U.S.A., received a telegram of congratulations from the National Endowment of the Arts in Washington, claiming him as a native son.

And the *Dorchester Signpost*, the tiny community newspaper back in the small town where she spent her teenage years, had no trouble at all understanding the event's significance. "Evelyn Hart," said the headline. "Best young dancer in the world."

Initially, Evelyn had trouble coming to terms with the fact that she had won at all. She came home from Varna very scared. So much had happened, so suddenly – such acclaim, such recognition – yet in her own eyes, she remained so deficient. Her technique was imperfect; her knowledge of the classics was minimal. She felt like an imposter. She had also been working at a manic pace to prepare herself for the competitions; now they were over, her nerves were raw and she was physically exhausted.

"A competition is not what dance is about," she told an interviewer soon after her return. "It's an indication of potential rather than an accomplishment."

Did she now plan, someone asked, to go to the Moscow competition, where Karen Kain and Frank Augustyn had been silver medallists?

"No, I've had it," she said. "I'd seen very few overseas dancers before this summer, and it was a good chance to see where I stand. It taught me that there are some technical things that I'll never do, and that my priorities are more artistic than technical."

How did it feel to be in a position to push Karen Kain from her perch as Canada's "première danseuse"?

"If that were to happen," she retorted, "it would be a great disappointment, because it would mean it could happen to me perhaps just as easily and readily . . . In Canadian ballet, there is certainly room for far more stars."

Would she and Peregrine be leaving the company now that they had won instant international fame?

DALE YOSHIDA

*A
shy smile
of triumph
as Evelyn arrives
home to cheers
and flowers
after her
Varna success,
1980.*

No, she said. That wasn't the point of entering the competitions. She had already signed a contract for the year and her personal loyalties were with the company. Peregrine said he wasn't ready to move on for at least two years.

She told me that October that while she no longer felt as closely attached to the company as she once had, the experience of Varna had shown her that "what's going on here [in Winnipeg] is very valid. I feel very strongly that I want to do most of my dancing *in* Canada *for* Canada. I'd like Canada to know that its artists are and can be comparable with any in the world."

She was also well aware of the protection that Winnipeg offered. The company structure gave her a place to discover her limits and explore her potential, without the stress that comes with being a stranger in a strange company. Just because she had won a competition didn't mean that she was suddenly ready to take on the world.

"It's very important for me not to get carried away," she said. "I can't feel I have to get perfect all of a sudden. I can't expect myself suddenly to be able to do thirty-two *fouettés* or leap higher just because I won a competition. The gold medal helps me realize I have things that I can do; it puts it all in perspective. I consider myself a lyric dancer, not a technical one. I don't consider myself deficient in technique, but I couldn't compare myself to someone who's born with feet and legs that let them jump, or to Ann Marie de Angelo and her spins. I consider myself a creator of illusion. However fast I move, I think I still come out lyrical."

Within twenty-four hours of their arrival home, Evelyn and Peregrine were in rehearsal again, with Frank Augustyn, preparing for their participation in a show called *Dance! Dance! Dance!* The show was produced by Vancouver promoter David Y. H. Lui to tour Alberta as part of the province's seventy-fifth anniversary celebrations in 1980. Initially, Evelyn had been scheduled to dance a new pas de deux with Augustyn by Caracas artistic director Vicente Nebrada, *A Dance for You*, but difficulties arose in rehearsal and Evelyn asked for a change of partner. It was the last pas de deux Evelyn and Peregrine learned together.

Lui had put the artistic roster together months previously. It included Evelyn, Peregrine, Augustyn, and Marianna Tcherkassky, a principal dancer with American Ballet Theatre, as Augustyn's partner. The program also featured Ulysses Dove and Donna Wood from the Alvin Ailey company in New York, ABT's Danilo Radojevic, ex-Joffrey principal Ann Marie de Angelo, and the recent Soviet defectors Leonid Koslov and his wife, Valentina Koslova.

The authorities in charge of the province's celebrations had looked askance at Lui's initial inclusion of Evelyn and Peregrine on such a high-profile bill, arguing that Albertans got to see the Winnipeg couple all the time, and it was at the province's insistence that the Russians were hired. As it happened, Evelyn and Peregrine made their first post-Varna appearances in Canada on that tour, and they stole the show.

That October, Winnipeg mayor Bill Norrie presented Evelyn, Peregrine, and Stafford with City of Winnipeg rings in honour of their artistic accomplishments in Osaka and Varna, and gave gold medallions for "outstanding achievement" to Spohr and Moroni. And in the season-opening performances at the Centennial Concert Hall, Evelyn and Peregrine performed *Belong* for the first time for their hometown audiences.

A capacity crowd roared to its feet in a standing ovation at the end of the performance and thronged the lobby to inspect a display-case housing the medals and the cable of congratulations from Trudeau. In *The Winnipeg Tribune*, critic Lynne Robson greeted *Belong* as a "stunningly beautiful" ballet, loved Evelyn's "incredible control and flexibility," and raved about Peregrine.

"A summer of successful competition obviously proved beneficial," she wrote. "He performed as Winnipeggers have never seen him perform before." She particularly liked his "new-found stage presence and dramatic flair" in the male solo in *Five Tangos*, and her enthusiasm was echoed by J. J. van Vlasselaer in *Le Droit* in Ottawa the following month. Peregrine, said the critic, "has suddenly found the ease, the aplomb, the élan that transforms a very good dancer into a presence."

During that late-fall tour of Eastern Canada and the U.S.A., the company returned to New York for performances at the new centre for the performing arts at Lehman College in the Bronx. Although the Bronx is normally off the beaten path for New York's dance critics, the Varna successes had made Evelyn a major attraction, and the heavyweight critical fraternity was much in evidence. They saw her perform both *Belong* and *A Dance for You* with Peregrine.

Jennifer Dunning in the *New York Times* called her "a dancer of great strength . . . she dances on the verge of the moment, her feet most often in half-point and not a listless muscle in her body, with lush, expansive arms that soften her somewhat distant look." Her look "of rapt, unconsummated attack" served her well in *Belong*, said Dunning. She also liked what the couple did in *A Dance for You*. "Another pas de deux of interrupted passion, it substituted spinning turns of all descriptions for Mr. Vesak's pullings-together and -apart, adding for effect such surprises as a floor slide, a wink and a one-armed lift that, to their credit, the two dancers never over-theatricalized."

In the *New York Post*, Clive Barnes called Evelyn "unquestionably a dancer of world class . . . Peregrine is a good partner with a lithe, athletic style, but Miss Hart is a gem. Her body and its placement is perfect, and she moves with a sort of grave, objective self-absorption, as if she was simply the instrument of dance. One must see her in other roles – her *Giselle* has been highly commended – but she has the ineffable image of greatness about her."

The Associated Press correspondent thought that watching *Belong* "was like watching a love-affair on stage." And the agency quoted Evelyn as saying: "We feel that way, hopefully, most of the time. Once the music starts, no matter what you feel inside, you sort of melt."

Well, maybe in public. "Harmony brings the BEST results," Spohr had written in his post-Varna circular letter, and on the surface, all seemed well in the Hart-Peregrine partnership. Talking about working with Evelyn on *Belong* in an interview on the CKND-TV film, Peregrine said: "I like her very much, so it's very easy to feel warm towards her: it's not a put-on feeling . . . When I can look at her in the middle of a pas de deux and I can feel that things are going well for her, and I can feel that we're together, feeling the music the same way, or that I'm feeling her rhythm while I'm partnering her, that's very special. When we have that contact between us it automatically has to be visible in the work that we do."

But behind the scenes, the relationship was steadily worsening. And Evelyn, watching it crumble, became increasingly worried that their success had locked them together. Hart and Peregrine in *Belong* – it was the company's ticket to success, and the company sold it hard. She began to cast around for alternatives, someone mature, someone who had been through the ballet mill and could help show her the way.

She had a sample of what might be possible that December, when Zane Wilson, principal dancer of the Ballet Internacional de Caracas, visited Winnipeg to perform in the RWB première of *Our Waltzes* by Caracas artistic director Vicente Nebrada.

For the first time, she danced with a partner who gave her a true sense of partnership on the stage – a true sense of instinctive performing harmony and unanimity. The wall between them melted away. It gave her confidence. When she dances with a partner who is that open and that supportive, she subsequently said, "I don't feel his hands touch me; but I'm very aware of the fact that I'm not out there alone . . . and that takes away the pressure . . . the trapdoor to my creativity opens."

Her search for partners who could make that essential connection has consumed much of her subsequent career.

Logically, Evelyn's career should have taken off into the stratosphere after Varna – and carried the company's future with it. Already she had achieved more than any other dancer from the West had ever achieved before, even eclipsing the successes of Kain and Augustyn at Moscow.

Spohr talked hopefully about the achievements in Osaka and Varna as "the beginning of another fantastic era for the Royal Winnipeg Ballet," and the company took every opportunity it could to display the sudden riches that had fallen into its lap. Publicist Lendre Rodgers (later Lendre Rodgers Kearns) marketed Evelyn so hard people began to call the company Rodgers and Hart. And the response at the box office showed a renewed audience enthusiasm that was clearly tied to the international successes. In the first post-Varna season, the company sold more seats than they had in a decade. The Christmas mixed-bill program, which traditionally alternates from year to year with *Nutcracker* (and traditionally sells fewer tickets), played to a mixed-bill all-time attendance record of 96 per cent. The winter series, in February and March, was tailored to showcase the medal-winners. The repertoire included a revival of Vesak's *Ecstasy of Rita Joe*, plus the world premières of a new Vesak work, *Meadow Dances*, and van Dantzig's *Moments Shared*. The series played to a 98 per cent capacity audience. General manager Bill Riske compared the period to the company's golden years of medal-winning successes in Europe in the late 1960s.

In retrospect, however, it is clear that the advantages for Evelyn were not pursued by the company as energetically as they might have been – nor did

DAVID COOPER

Evelyn and David Peregrine in Rudi van Dantzig's Moments Shared, *a gift from the choreographer in 1979.*

the international invitations pour in as lavishly as the Winnipeggers might have hoped. When Kain and Augustyn came back from Moscow with their silver medals, the National Ballet's glossy and experienced publicity machinery, operating in the same city as the country's principal national media, made them into stars. In Evelyn's company, the machinery was neither as sophisticated, nor was it located in Toronto.

But Evelyn was also at that time lacking the guidance of a personal manager, a person with connections who would be able to devote his energies to engineering the kind of image-building guest-appearance invitations that would give her optimum exposure and experience.

These deficiencies may have been blessings in disguise. Although she told me as early as October of 1980 that she wanted the experience of travelling abroad to learn new roles, she was almost certainly not ready to have the trials of international stardom thrust upon her so suddenly. Her partnership with

Peregrine was still causing her anxiety, and she felt increasingly under pressure to live up to some kind of "gold medallist" image, which sapped her already uncertain confidence as an artist even further. Varna had given her encouragement to pursue her ambitions for stardom, but she constantly felt that she wasn't living up to other people's expectations. She judged herself against the stars she met, and found herself wanting. She was convinced that she was less than world class in her technique – she didn't have a high jump, she didn't have a great turn, she didn't have a high extension, she didn't like her feet. So what if she had expressive powers that were virtually unmatchable anywhere? She had always been told that no dancer could have both brilliant technique and brilliant artistry, but she wanted both. To Evelyn, the expressiveness that is her greatest strength is no virtue at all without perfect technique; it's setting an intangible quality against tangible skills. Who cares?

Well, a lot of people cared. In March 1981 she and Peregrine danced *Belong* in a National Ballet of Canada fund-raising gala in Toronto, and once again she stole the show in a program that included Carla Fracci, Erik Bruhn, and Ib Andersen (three glamorous international stars) dancing *La Sylphide*.

The casting for *La Sylphide* was what drew the New York critics to Toronto, but it was Evelyn and Peregrine they stayed to praise. Clive Barnes in the *New York Post* called them the hit of the evening. Anna Kisselgoff in the *New York Times* said they "deserved every iota" of their standing ovation. "Both dance," she wrote, "with the fluency the National Ballet's style discourages." And in *The Globe and Mail* Stephen Godfrey said, "the sheer beauty of line in their dancing provided the most memorable images of the evening; three curtain-calls later, the audience still sounded as if it wanted to see them again."

For Evelyn, this return in triumph to Toronto – the city that had rejected her – had a special sweetness.

Two months later, she strengthened another connection with the National Ballet of Canada: her friendship with ballerina Veronica Tennant, the dancer who had been Evelyn's first inspiration.

It happened at a gala at the National Arts Centre in Ottawa that May. Canada's eight leading ballet and modern dance companies were brought together by the Canadian Association of Professional Dance Organizations for a Canadian dance spectacular. It was, for Canadian dance, a historic moment. It was the first time this type of gathering had been organized on such a scale, and it was a visible demonstration of the astonishing growth that had characterized the art of dance in Canada in the previous quarter-century.

However, for Evelyn, who was there to dance with Peregrine and RWB company members in Nebrada's *Our Waltzes*, the value was not so much historical as personal. Veronica had spotted Evelyn years before in a perform- ance in Montreal, soon after she had joined the RWB, and had gone backstage to tell "this wonderful, vivacious, bubbly young girl" how much she enjoyed her dancing. Later, when Evelyn won the gold medal at Varna, Veronica recognized the name and wrote to congratulate her, and a sporadic corre- spondence began. But it wasn't until the CAPDO gala that their friendship was really sealed.

To Veronica, who was there to dance Juliet in the ballroom scene from Cranko's *Romeo and Juliet* – the ballet that had first inspired the young Evelyn – Evelyn's performance in *Our Waltzes* embodied the spirit of the dance. "I just remember a shimmer," she says. "I don't remember the ballet, even the style; she just struck me." Afterward, she always thought of Evelyn whenever she needed inspiration before going on for a performance – "not in any way to emulate or copy or reproduce, but just to see that that there is someone who is able to take one's dreams and realize them."

In the summer of 1981, Evelyn and Peregrine returned to Japan to dance as guests in a "Ballet Fantasy" program with the Homura Tomoi Ballet in Tokyo. They danced *Belong* and the *Nutcracker* pas de deux together. Evelyn also danced the *Giselle* pas de deux with company principal Makio Homura, and Peregrine performed the *Le Corsaire* pas de deux with another principal, Toyoko Miyamoto. They had exactly four days to prepare for the week of performances, and they were paid the princely sum of $1,500 each. The audiences loved them. For Evelyn, it was the first of many guest appearances in a country that she has come to love.

However, she was increasingly in need of inspiration at home. The problem of repertoire loomed especially large. When she was dancing in Osaka, a Hungarian competitor asked what roles she danced, and she had nothing to tell the girl. Her loyalty to the company was not in question, but in interviews immediately after the Varna success she had made no secret of her hopes that the company would begin to acquire a full-length classical repertoire, which would allow her to develop her own classical technique, stamina, and inter- pretive strength.

The classics, she realized, were her true home. "Not tragedy, necessarily," she told me, "but anything that deals with basic human love, that touches the human spirit." It was all very well to dance *Five Tangos* – she found it exciting, but it didn't plumb the depths she was searching for. The difference between the great classics and a work like *Five Tangos*, she said, was like the difference between "a passionate love-affair and an ongoing relationship over twenty years." One doesn't reach the same depths as the other.

Spohr, listening carefully to his star, had dropped hints that something big was on the way. And as the company's 1980-81 season approached its end, he announced it would be giving the North American première of Rudi van Dantzig's *Romeo and Juliet* to open its season the following fall.

Evelyn partnered Makio Homura in the Giselle *second-act pas de deux during performances with the Homura Tomoi Ballet in Tokyo in 1981.*

T. ITOGA

Evelyn and David Peregrine in Rudi van Dantzig's Romeo and Juliet, *given its
North American première by the* RWB *in October, 1981.*

DAVID COOPER

5 *Dream into Nightmare*

Spohr's decision to mount a full-scale, full-length production of *Romeo and Juliet* was not greeted with enthusiasm in all quarters. The RWB had built its reputation as a compact, easily transportable company of about two dozen dancers – a dance commando force, as someone once described it – with a repertoire of an almost ridiculous diversity. Something for everyone had been its key programming principle since the days of its founding in 1939; it was a principle Spohr had always professed to follow. Yet now he was proposing to move the company in the direction of the full-length classics, a field that had, by unspoken agreement, been dominated in Canada until that time by the National Ballet of Canada – a company with both the financial and the human resources to stage these mammoth extravaganzas.

The Canada Council viewed the move as questionable, and one that might establish a dangerous precedent. It was not about to encourage such foolhardiness by increasing the company's annual grant. But Spohr argued that the classical repertoire was something he had always dreamed of for the company. Now, thanks to the work of the school, he finally had a company that could handle these works properly. And riding the crest of a wave of Hart-induced popularity that saw the company close the 1980-81 season with a surplus of $120,000 and enter the next with a new high in subscriptions, he financed the $250,000 production of *Romeo* in part from the company's own accumulated surplus.

The RWB had, in fact, regularly presented one highly successful full-length ballet, John Neumeier's *Nutcracker*, since 1973. But it was obvious that a major factor in Spohr's decision to increase the company's repertoire of full-length classics was the emergence of Evelyn into the international eye. It was also time for her to move on as an artist. She was twenty-five, an age at which many other ballerinas had already been dancing Giselle and Swan Queen roles for years. Yet all she had in the classical compartment of her artistic quiver was Louise in *Nutcracker* and a few snippets of pas de deux. She had already made it plain that she wanted the big roles; it was the only way she would grow as an interpretive artist. The unspoken implication was obvious: if she didn't get that chance in Winnipeg, she would look elsewhere. To Spohr and his cohorts, that was unthinkable. For all his protests about the company's readiness, Spohr was effectively backed into the decision to go to the full-length works by Evelyn.

Fortunately, the pressure came at the right time. Through the steady development by Moroni of the professional program of the school, he found himself well supplied with high-quality student talent to supplement the company for the crowd scenes and group dances, just as he already did for the biennial Christmas *Nutcracker*. And through his recent connections with the Dutch school of choreography, he had won the goodwill and interest of Rudi van Dantzig, who was, in any case, infatuated with Evelyn's talent.

The RWB production of van Dantzig's *Romeo and Juliet* was the North American première of a work first seen in Holland with the Dutch National Ballet in 1965. Although van Dantzig adapted it to reduce the crowd scenes and to give dancers multiple minor roles, it was still the biggest production in the company's history to that date, using all twenty-four of the company's dancers, as well as twelve students from the professional division of the school and three members of the artistic staff. Van Dantzig and his regisseur, Sonia Marchiolli, spent a month with the company in the spring of 1981, then returned for a further six weeks prior to the opening in the fall. It took the wardrobe department five months to build the 130 costumes.

For Evelyn, the work period with van Dantzig was a time of mixed emotions. She found him quite specific in his manner of working, and she did her best to produce what he asked without much in the way of personal input from herself. "The way you can help him best is by being close to his image," she says. "So your own sense of self doesn't come into it. Yet what's so funny is the little note he wrote to me after, talking about our wonderful co-creation, Juliet. I didn't feel I was creating. I felt all I was doing was being guided."

On the personal side, however, there was a part of her that loved him very dearly when they first came together. She loved the soft-spoken, boyish van

Dantzig's lyrical manner of choreographing. And naturally courteous, professionally admiring, he treated her like a star.

The adoration was not something he had to work at. During his visit to Winnipeg in the 1979-80 season to mount *Four Last Songs*, he had given her the pas de deux *Moments Shared*, because he enjoyed working with her so much and a gift would enable him to work with her a little longer. He saw her as his ideal dancer, one who enabled all his dreams to come true. He compared her musicality and spirituality to Ulanova's, and it is possible to find close parallels between what he made Evelyn do as Juliet and what Ulanova does in her own film version of the role. "For me," he said, "Ulanova was one of the unearthly people. Evelyn is like that – in a world, in a class, of her own. She doesn't dance or act Juliet, she becomes her."

He loved the intensity of her performance. The intensity of her perfectionism, on the other hand, gave him cause for concern.

She had managed to get her hands on a key that allowed her access to the studio after hours, and she habitually spent all her free time there. (To avoid detection she would practise with the lights out.) On the Sunday morning of the opening week, van Dantzig found her curled up, exhausted, in a seat at the theatre, listening to an orchestral run-through of Prokofiev's music for the ballet. Worried about the effects of strain, he and designer Toer van Schayk forbade her to go to the studio that day and insisted instead that she go with them for a drive in the countryside.

The performances were tense. The hometown critics loved Evelyn. Watching Hart and Peregrine mature from shy children to suicidal lovers, said Lynne Robson in the *Winnipeg Free Press*, "demonstrates their growth in dramatic talent during the last two years. Hart has been an excellent dancer longer than she's been a good actress. Last night her plight brought tears to many eyes."

But some of the out-of-towners in for the première were less impressed. Evelyn's Juliet, said John Ayre in *Maclean's*, was "more like tragic divorcée than innocent teenager. Unquestionably, however, there was a strong base of dramatic substance and energy that waited for more settled nights." Stephen Godfrey, in *The Globe and Mail*, said she appeared to be "a natural actress, but not, at this point, a dancing one. Her lush, dancing Juliet abstracts the emotion to the extent that when a long, curved arm melts into Romeo's back on a musical phrase one can easily forget it is meant to be a passionate embrace. On the other hand, her acting, with its incredibly sharp head movements, is marked by febrile, whippet-like reflexes, as if this Juliet appears moved by neither thought nor emotion, but nervous impulses."

At the time, the negative reviews stung. What hurt her most was not the fact that they criticized the way she danced – she knew she would make progress

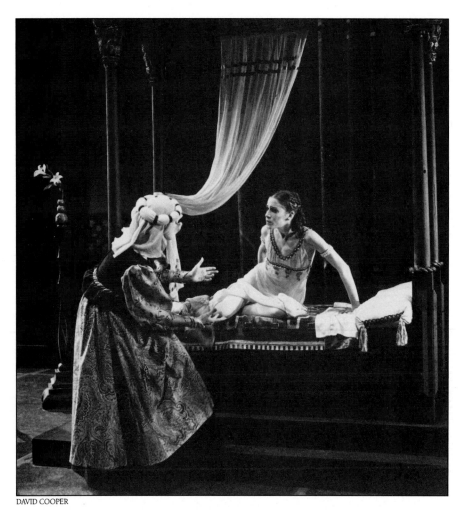

DAVID COOPER

Evelyn as Juliet with Cathy Taylor as the Nurse in the RWB's production of Romeo and Juliet.

from year to year, and the Juliet she performed at the age of twenty-five was very different from the Juliet she would offer at thirty. What bothered her was the thought that she wasn't able to make Juliet live for that particular individual; communication and sharing remained the key to her art.

The production itself won widespread acclaim. Ayre said in *Maclean's*, "The astonishing vibrancy and success of this production has embarrassing implications. With its own money, a small ballet company has mounted a classic with greater dramatic flair than anything the National Ballet has done in years." The National, he said, "must be wondering about its mandate."

Clement Crisp, writing for London's *Financial Times*, caught up with the company on tour in Vancouver, and saw Evelyn dance in both *Romeo and Juliet* and a mixed bill. He called her "the company's jewel . . . Slender, elegant and harmonious in physique, easy in technique, she combines a poetic dreaminess with flashes of extreme passion, and seems to dance for the sake of the dance itself. In *Our Waltzes*, she is a flame in a red dress, and in one number shows so bold a physical presence that, given a passing facial resemblance, I thought to see the young Plisetskaya again.

"As Juliet . . . she is exquisite . . . luminous, passionate . . . As the child Juliet I found her too vivacious, but once love has struck, she enters the soul of the character. Her body drifts, hovers over the dances – she must be one of nature's Giselles – and suddenly plunges deep into Juliet's emotions. I thought hers a beautiful interpretation, and one well supported by her Romeo, David Peregrine, who exemplified the good technical manners and the direct, uncomplicated dramatic style of the Winnipeg male contingent."

Plisetskaya. Ulanova. The comparisons with the great ones were piling up for the girl Spohr had called "Little Miss Leningrad." And it was hardly a coincidence that the comparisons involved Russian dancers. It was the Russian style, with its expressive arm movements and its rushing passions, to which she was drawn. It was the Russian style to which she had been exposed through the imported Vaganova teachers at the school and company. And it was the Russian style that had made such an impression on her during the two international competitions. Later, she would express preferences for one aspect of this style over another; the style of Leningrad's Kirov Ballet, which is widely regarded as the shrine of the purest of all ballet techniques, would, interestingly enough, take second place in her estimation to the style of the Bolshoi Ballet in Moscow. But for the time being, at least, such subtleties of differentiation were for the future.

In November 1981, a month after the Winnipeg opening of *Romeo and Juliet*, Evelyn found a new idol – the Brazil-born dancer Marcia Haydée, acclaimed as one of the world's great dance actresses during her years as prima ballerina at the Stuttgart Ballet in the 1960s and 1970s, and artistic director at Stuttgart since 1976.

They met when they appeared on the same program at a gala to celebrate the fifteenth anniversary of the Alberta Ballet, in Edmonton. Haydée and Richard Cragun, her partner from the Stuttgart Ballet, were the gala's main attraction. They performed an ebullient pas de deux from John Cranko's *The Taming of the Shrew* and a frothy divertissement by the Brazilian choreographer Dalah Aschar. But Evelyn, performing *Belong* with Peregrine, was counted by many in the throng of dance-world luminaries from New York and Toronto as an equal draw.

Haydée was a dancer whom the Carters, back in London, used to hold up to

Evelyn as an example of a model for her own dancing – not the greatest technique in the world, but enormously expressive. Watching Haydée do the comic *Shrew* pas de deux on that Edmonton stage, Evelyn suddenly realized she was looking at "the first dancer to really touch me. The curtain went up and it was as if this light came out of her. As I watched her from the wings, I felt I would be quite content to be behind her. I would die to be a tree at the side of the stage when she was dancing. I felt this, and I was really taken aback by it. The ambition for myself was gone and in its place was an ambition for quality; for the sake of the art."

The admiration was mutual. As Cragun recalls it, after *Belong* "we both went to Evelyn, and Marcia said, 'You are the most divine creature I've ever seen,' and Evelyn said 'Oh, but Marcia, *you* are the most incredible woman I've ever seen.' Each was fascinated with the other person, but it was for real. They were absolutely sincere."

When the company toured *Romeo and Juliet* to eastern Canada the following spring, the mixed reception continued. Linde Howe-Beck, in Montreal's *The Gazette*, thought neither dancer "managed to convey the deep joy and torment that is at the core of the ballet." In *The Citizen*, Jacob Siskind blamed the production itself for the fact that the company "falls short of the mark it has set itself . . . There was no romance, no mystery, no sense of discovery, and certainly no feeling of tragedy at the end. The two lovers were pleasant enough people who kept rushing hither and yon across the stage with their arms outspread, flapping about more like a pair of homing pigeons looking for their roost than eager, excited, teenaged would-be lovers."

Rebecca Robinson, reviewing the same performance for the *Ottawa Revue*, said that "even with the extraordinary gifts of ballet's most exquisite instrument, Evelyn Hart, the romantic pas de deux were too insipid, at best merely pretty." However, she said, it is "never disappointing" to see Evelyn Hart. "With most dancers, no matter how graceful the head or limpid the arms, we are reminded of the existence of gravity in their torsos and legs. Not so with Hart, for here we have no arms and legs, just four ethereal limbs, equally weightless, floating free like the tendrils of a sea anemone wafted on the invisible currents of the ocean. Juliet is Hart's first major role. Shakespeare's heroine met an untimely end, but fortunately for us, Juliet's end marks Hart's beginning – and there's just no end in sight."

Van Dantzig recognized the complaints, but says, "Evelyn was my Juliet, for sure – incredibly serious, and sometimes I was criticized for that, for letting it be too dramatic. Already from a young girl she seemed to have fate inside her.

But that was what I had in mind. She was different from others. When she gave her heart she gave her whole being."

That sense of commitment has always been crucial to Evelyn's success as a performer, and from *Romeo and Juliet* on it was to draw increasing comment. As she became more familiar with the major roles, she began to realize that she was more than a choreographer's tool. While she felt a responsibility to the artistic wishes of the choreographer, she also felt she had much of her own to share. Striking that balance between faithful replication and personal input would be an important part of her battle as an artist.

Meanwhile, her professional relationship with Peregrine gave her continuing concern.

Lendre Rodgers Kearns recalls taking Evelyn and Peregrine to New York in the period of preparation for *Romeo and Juliet* for a photocall for a *Dance Magazine* cover. Relations had become so bad that neither dancer was talking to the other. Kearns arranged to get them all separate seats on the airplane, with an empty seat beside her so they could take turns coming to visit. All weekend she took turns chaperoning the pair – "I take David for breakfast, I take Evelyn for breakfast. I take David for lunch, I take Evelyn for lunch. I ate six meals a day, and I couldn't even tell them what I was doing with the other one. It was hysterical."

In Kearns's view, dance was not Peregrine's priority; success was. But he wasn't prepared to match Evelyn's commitment and personal investment in the work. Evelyn felt the same. It seemed to her that she was getting nothing back from him when they worked together on the stage; she would arrive ready for work, and all he would want to do was practise his pirouettes. It reached the point where he hadn't even warmed up when he came to work. It was clear to Evelyn that a break had to come.

Unfortunately, she began to break up the partnership at precisely the period at which Peregrine was beginning to feel he was achieving the kind of results in his career that he had always dreamed of. The successes at Osaka and Varna had catapulted the two of them to international acclaim, and he was ready to dance *Belong* (the basis on which all that success had been built) as long as audiences wanted to see it.

Romeo was his next big step as an artist. It was his first full-length role, and he revelled in the challenge, though he warned an interviewer that his version of the character "cannot satisfy everyone . . . Romeo is far more impetuous than I am. I tend to reflect on things. I don't like to jump onto a bandwagon before inspecting it thoroughly. Because Romeo is so impetuous his life is very exhilarating . . . very breathtaking."

He drew parallels between Romeo's impetuosity and his own hobby, flying his light airplane. "Whenever I fly or whenever I do leaps or spins on stage, I have an exhilarating feeling of freedom," he said. "I think that is how Romeo went through life. What Romeo didn't have that is absolutely essential to the dancer and the pilot is an underlying sense of control. Romeo's life was like a roller coaster. It was filled with incredible thrills, but he had little real control over them. That is why his life was a tragedy."

It is significant, though, that even at that early stage, in the fall of 1981, Peregrine was already talking about extending his performing career into acting, either on stage or film. One of his favourite novels, Frank Herbert's *Dune*, was at that time being prepared for the screen. Fancying the central role and believing it would suit a dancer, he called Herbert at home, offered him tickets to an RWB show, and bent the writer's ear about the casting. Herbert said he had nothing to do with the casting, but added that in his opinion the character would have to be played by someone with hawk-like features. "I asked him if a hawk-like name would do," said Peregrine. "I think I struck out. He didn't catch my joke and he didn't catch my show."

Evelyn, meanwhile, had begun a descent down a spiral of despair that would become a major emotional crisis. Despite her international successes, her attachment to Winnipeg continued to keep her from taking the leap forward that many thought she should take. The reasons for that reluctance were complex: fear of the unknown, lack of confidence in herself as a performer, the sheer convenience of not having to make decisions about repertoire, tours, and performances, and genuine regard for the Winnipeg company.

She liked the RWB's "particularly human feel," a warmth that she hadn't found in companies elsewhere. She was proud, too, of the way the company had created itself from nothing in a small city on the Prairies. But she also felt a weighty responsibility. The reason she became upset and hysterical so often in the rehearsal room, she told me late in 1983, was not because she was worrying about herself but because she was worrying about the whole future of the company. Watching a rehearsal, she'd assume responsibility for its performance standards herself. The daily routine of compromise that is often the only way a performance reaches the stage offended her desire for perfection.

Yet in this place with which her life and career were so inextricably interwoven, she now felt a terrible isolation. No one, Evelyn least of all, had the slightest idea of how to handle the talent that had been revealed in the company's midst. Had there been anyone in place with some experience of dealing with that kind of success, the story might have been different. As it was everyone was learning as they went along, and inventing most of it.

Her two most significant relationships were drifting toward shipwreck. Moroni had receded into the background of her life, and the partnership with Peregrine was in serious question.

She felt as if everything was on her own slender shoulders. She had days of deep depression, usually triggered by the frustrations and the solitude – days when she could hardly see, set in a blackness so deep it seemed to suck her in.

Zane Wilson returned as a guest in March 1982 for the Winnipeg première of Vicente Nebrada's *Lento a Tempo e Appassionato*. It was a huge success. He came back in May to join her in the world première of Nebrada's *Firebird*. The piece drew mixed reviews, but John Ayre in *Maclean's* called Evelyn's dancing and acting a tour de force, and said she "set a new standard for the often-trifling firebird role. In a crimson, flame-peaked helmet and red body stocking, Hart carried the firebird into the surrealistic realm of the Swan Queen."

But the albatross of *Belong* continued to hang about her neck. On tour in eastern Canada that February and March, she and Peregrine were made to dance it repeatedly, and audiences and critics continued to rave, which made matters worse. They danced it in Ottawa for a gala before the Queen in April. In May they won ACTRA awards for their part in the CKND-TV post-Varna *Belong* special, and the following week made their London debut dancing *Belong* before Princess Margaret at a fund-raising gala for Sadler's Wells Theatre. It earned them four curtain-calls on a packed program where the other calls were held rigorously to two and occasionally three.

She grew further and further from the work. "Am I a rounded artist or just the female half of *Belong*?" she asked one interviewer. "You like to think you've got other things to offer an audience. I could grow more in it artistically if I did it less frequently." And she told Stephen Godfrey, "I understand the reasons for doing it so often, but sometimes I feel like saying 'Give me a break.' As soon as I think it's being done instead of trying something new, I'll stop."

But in his review a week later, Godfrey wrote: "Judging by the standing ovation that greeted the performance of the dance by her and David Peregrine . . . she should reconsider . . . *Belong* remains a great star vehicle, a galvanizing piece of dance and, not incidentally, a show-stopper. Dances like that are hard to find."

Others agreed. William Littler, in *The Toronto Star*, said "it is not a great piece of choreography . . . but it flows. God, does it flow. And Hart and Peregrine flow with it so completely, with such a unanimous sense of line, that the two of them seem almost to possess the same body. Their achievement, in essence, is a distillation of lyricism."

Despite her public protests, it wasn't the ballet itself that was the root of the the problem. The partnership was at crisis point.

Her determination to find herself a new partner – someone she could grow with – had become an obsession. It had also clarified in her mind exactly what she wanted from a partnership. It was a vision closely linked to her ideal of total commitment to the dance. A performer, she believed, should never be an actor; a performer should just *be*. It was a matter of spontaneity and relaxation – but, just as important, it demanded a matching commitment from the partner, a mutuality of minds. "It's like going to the nude beach. It doesn't work if only one of you undresses."

This kind of paragon, as she was to continue to discover, was hard to find. For a time, she wondered if something permanent in terms of a dance partnership might evolve with Frank Augustyn. She danced with him first in 1980, when he coached her for her trips to Osaka and Varna, and later when she appeared as a guest with the National Ballet of Canada. They fitted well in size, and looked good together on the stage. She was also more than a little taken with him as an individual – "Karen [Kain] said once, you can always count on Frank for a laugh. He has a boyishness and a childishness in him that is so much fun to be with. He can be very sophisticated and debonair and do all that stuff, and he has such a sense of the artist about him, but there is also a side of him that can be an absolute kid."

As a partner, he was always considerate, but very much in command. He had been trained in one balletic school, Evelyn in another, and he would try to retrain her technically – suggesting changes in her *fouetté* turn, for instance. She never thought she was good enough for him. But she recognized his values, and appreciated what he did for her.

"The one thing I always treasured about Frank was his understanding that a real partner, whatever he does, can enhance the whole thing. He's not just there for the turns. Frank had a real pride in the little tricks that he had in *Giselle*, creating this effect of lightness – it's wonderful to work with someone like that. He taught me a lift that we did in Varna, and when we did it they applauded because they'd never seen it done like that before."

Rudi van Dantzig invited her to Amsterdam to dance as a guest with his company that spring, and she thought the invitation might lead to a permanent guest relationship with the Dutch National.

She was by no means convinced that Amsterdam would be the best place to be. People had warned her that life in the company was riddled with dance politics. She thought she might prefer Stuttgart, where Marcia Haydée was in control and Cragun was a principal dancer. Still, she reasoned, Amsterdam would certainly be a useful toehold in Europe, and she was intrigued enough by van Dantzig's mind, personality, and style to think it might be interesting to be the instrument of his vision.

In fact he went even further, asking her to join the company on a full-time basis, at the same time warning her that the treatment she would receive would be very different from her experiences in Winnipeg. The struggle, he told her, would be harder.

Evelyn, ever-loyal to Winnipeg and probably frightened by the thought of having to release her grip on her one point of security and stability, turned him down.

However, it was through Rudi van Dantzig's invitation to Amsterdam that Evelyn met a dancer who was to have an even more profound influence on her career and her life than van Dantzig – Henny Jurriens.

They first met in the studio of the Dutch National Ballet. Jurriens, the leading principal dancer with the company, was nervous. Van Dantzig had asked him to dance *Moments Shared* with the Varna gold medallist, a girl from Winnipeg. Jurriens had had only four days to learn the piece – the young Luc Amyot, who had been scheduled to perform with Evelyn, had been injured, and Jurriens, who had been home with the 'flu, had been called in to take over.

Evelyn was already in the studio when Jurriens arrived for their first rehearsal. "You know how you have a few moments in your life that when you think of it you see the picture?" he subsequently recalled. "I came in, she turned round and said, 'You must be Henny,' and she ran to me and jumped into my arms. And from the moment we touched each other it clicked straight away."

They did *Moments Shared* and *Four Last Songs*. Until that time, he had looked on *Moments Shared* as just another boring pas de deux. But when he started working with her it all made sense. "Suddenly there was musicality in there. Until then I never worked in a such a musical way; you never aimed for a certain note, you just hoped you hit the note. She changed that. For each note she had a movement. Now I don't understand how I could have worked the way I did before."

In the spring of 1982, Evelyn finally acquired what she had been needing since Varna – a manager. Charles (Chuck) Marahrens was a former investment banker from New York, just entering the arts management business. His company, Corsair Productions, was already handling a number of other dancers of international repute, among them Patrick Bissell and others from American Ballet Theatre, and Vanessa Harwood and others from the National Ballet of Canada. According to RWB tour director Mark Porteous he was "a very untypical New York agent, which was part of the attraction . . . He quickly understood she was not the type who wanted to run after every single guest engagement that brought in big U.S. bucks, and he was agreeable to managing her that way."

He was taken on as much to bring some kind of coherence to the flood of invitations that Evelyn was now receiving as to generate work for her. He was also a useful buffer for her insecurities, accompanying her on her increasingly frequent guest trips abroad. But still there hovered *Belong* and the vexatious partnership. That summer, she and Peregrine were made to perform it again when the company went on tour to Greece and Cyprus. An Athens critic declared "I don't think we've ever seen such an exciting pas de deux in Greece." But Clement Crisp, who trailed the company loyally round the Mediterranean, reserved most of his praise for Evelyn for her performance in *Our Waltzes*. He called her "a ballerina whose radiant clarity is here all joy and innocent pleasure. It is a special delight to see how she inhabits the music, her body opening out in lovely curves, buoyed up on the almost too ingratiating melodic line".

When she danced, the image was all success. The human facts were a different matter.

NICK A. SARABANOS

Evelyn and David Peregrine perform Norbert Vesak's Belong, *during the 1982 RWB tour of Greece.*

Lendre Rodgers Kearns always believed David Moroni wanted Evelyn and Peregrine to be a couple because David Moroni had made them a couple, not because they were a good couple. "Maybe when they were students that was really logical, but it didn't take long to figure out that this was not a marriage made in heaven, and that with their motivations and their styles of working they were only going to be destructive to each other. But it took a lot of balls on Evelyn's part to be able to stand up to him and say, 'No, I'm not even going to stay in the same room with this guy.'"

The differences in their styles of working, in their approaches to dance, were easy to see. Peregrine liked the exciting, masculine aspect of dancing. Evelyn preferred precision, subtlety, quiet expressiveness. More important even than that, though, was the question of his commitment, itself connected to an essentially different worldview from Evelyn's. Maxine Hart has always believed Evelyn's expectations of her partners to be too great. "I really used to feel sorry for David Peregrine," she says. "I'm sure he tried his very best. But anyone who can go out and take flying lessons knows there's more to life than dancing."

Certainly, Peregrine had a lively interest in non-dance matters. Deeply serious in his intellectual pursuits, he read widely and argued vigorously, always ready to hear a new viewpoint. One of his most cherished memories was the day he met René Lévesque. On tour, he often disappeared on free days, opting to skip organized company outings in foreign cities in favour of private explorations. Many of his closest relationships had no connection with the world of ballet.

Whatever the differences, they intensified Evelyn's awareness of the need for more exposure and different partners. And she had reached a point at which the company was prepared to listen. There had been times when she had been ready to leave – times when she had to "create an emergency," as she put it, to get things done the way she wanted them done. But the people who ran the company knew how valuable she was to its continuing successes, and they had learned to compromise and accommodate. If she had an artistic problem she wanted to talk about, they'd listen. And the same applied to her increasing unhappiness about her partnership with Peregrine. General manager Bill Riske even set aside a package of money as insurance against the time when they might need to bring in someone new in a hurry.

Rudi van Dantzig was shocked at the harshness of Evelyn's demands to be released from her partnership with Peregrine. "He worked very conscientiously on the Romeo; I was not displeased at all. I am not sure where the friction started, but I saw him sometimes crying. He was very depressed, saying, she hates me."

Hatred wasn't the right word. Certainly, though, she was impatient to move on. *Romeo and Juliet* had given her a new vision of what she might be able to achieve on the stage. She was eager to pursue it. And when the break did finally come, it happened, says Evelyn, as much for the company as for herself. "There was also a regret that things could not be resolved," she says. "But, analyzing it, I knew that I had done everything I could do. I can't chastise myself."

Early in the fall of 1982, Evelyn was invited by Francia Russell at Pacific North West Ballet in Seattle to appear as a guest dancing the Black Swan pas de deux from *Swan Lake*. She was reluctant to tell Peregrine because she didn't want to have to perform with him. But inevitably he heard about it, and when she told him she was to dance with one of the Seattle principals and not with him his response was, she recalls, "almost belligerent."

His dissatisfaction was mirrored in the attitude of the artistic staff; it was almost as if it was her *duty* to take him with her. They were the RWB stars, and they were inseparable. Did she want to jeopardize all that had been achieved?

"I used to think she was going to explode," says Kearns. "Evelyn had always had her highs and her lows, but at least she had always had a middle ground where she lived, but it was getting to the point that the highs were becoming so infrequent, and the lows so consistent, that there was no time in the middle ground any more. It was absolutely terrifying."

At this period, according to Kearns, Evelyn's favourite avoidance technique for getting out of going to receptions after performances was to say she couldn't go because she had a run in her pantyhose. So Kearns kept her star in pantyhose; when she was shopping, she'd buy an extra pair and tuck them in her purse. If this wasn't possible, she'd wash her own out in the bathroom and have them dry by the end of the show.

More seriously, it was becoming increasingly difficult to get Evelyn onto the stage. She needed constant reassurance before performance. "When she really hit the rockiest of times in terms of the rollercoaster, it used to be like tag team time," says Kearns. "Arnold would come flying, looking for me, I'd go in and do the first phase, then I'd tag out to Mark and he'd be in, then he'd tag out to me and I'd be in."

In the end, Evelyn turned down the Seattle invitation, because her inability to do the requisite thirty-two *fouettés* in the Black Swan pas de deux made her feel inadequate. (*Fouettés*, whipping kicks while turning on the spot, have never been Evelyn's forté. She calls them "stupid work.") She spent the early fall under a cloud of guilt and contrition, working on the pas de deux for the season's opening performance in Winnipeg that October.

Her partner was soloist Baxter Branstetter, who was dancing with her frequently at this time. They worked initially under the tutelage of regisseur Alla Savchenko but switched later (which raised eyebrows in the company) to Galina Yordanova, who had begun to work with the company as a guest teacher. In the midst of this, Francia Russell arrived to spend a week preparing George Balanchine's *Allegro Brillante*, in which Evelyn and Branstetter were to dance the lead.

Evelyn, faced with the prospect of the two premières and still furious at what she felt was emotional blackmail over Peregrine, went into serious panic – a panic not helped by Spohr's critical comments on her performance at the dress rehearsal. She made it through the opening nights ("the scariest experience I had ever had; I lived through it barely") but at the Saturday matinée, as the stage manager called "Places, please" for the Black Swan pas de deux, she found herself transfixed, unable to make her way to the wings.

"Until then there had always been histrionics, but once she hit the stage she was fine," says Kearns, "so you knew there was this ritual to be performed, personally draining but worth the emotional investment. That day, we had gone through the whole ritual, the show was on, it was ten minutes before intermission, she was on right after. This was the point usually where she got left alone. As it happened, Mark and I were having people over for dinner, he had stuff to do at work, I had things to do at the market. So Mark heads off to the office, I head off to the market, both of us are gone . . . and disaster strikes. She doesn't go on. Intermission is over, the audience is back in its seats, and she's in hysterics, she's in tears, no one is going to get her on. And they didn't. By the time Mark and I got back it was all over."

They found her in the dressing room in uncontrollable floods of tears. A doctor was sent for; tranquillizers were prescribed. Soon after, with the encouragement of Porteous and Kearns, Evelyn began to see a psychiatrist.

The challenges continued to mount. Within days of the last of the Winnipeg shows that October, the company was due to leave for London, West Germany, Egypt, and Northern Ireland. Inspired by the audience response in Greece the previous summer, it was the company's first extensive tour outside North America since touring South America in 1975, and its first appearance in London in seventeen years – a big, image-building event.

Evelyn claims Spohr had made a pact with her that she wouldn't be asked to dance *Belong*, which was scheduled for performance throughout Europe, though even before the Winnipeg openings publicity material claimed she and Peregrine would be performing it for a BBC-TV film. Evelyn, yielding to pressure, agreed to do it a limited number of times, and in London it became, in the words of Mary Clarke in *The Guardian*, "the hit of the evening . . . A crowd-pleaser, expertly done."

For Germany, she had persuaded the company to bring in Zane Wilson to partner her in *Lento*. However, Wilson was injured and wasn't able to make it, so, once again, it was Hart and Peregrine. By that time, their relationship had reached the point where they wouldn't even say hello to each other before they went on for *Belong*. Evelyn would lie down at the centre of the stage for the opening position, and Peregrine would hover at the back, practising his pirouettes, refusing to lie down beside her until the lights dimmed for the opening of the piece.

The tension still didn't show. A German critic praised their "sensuous, smooth body language, full of poetry and erotic radiance." In Belfast, the *Irish Times* said they "brought a magic to the melting flow of movement . . . seeming at times to become a single expressive figure."

The company itself had mixed success in London. Critics found much to complain about in both its choice of repertoire and its dancing. But for Evelyn the trip was another personal triumph. Clement Crisp, still following the company for London's *Financial Times*, continued to rave about her work in *Our Waltzes*. He wrote that her "ability to play with the dance, to colour it with delicious nuances of feeling, has a vividness which owes little to her red dress, but everything to her glowing temperament, to her musicality, and that ardent lyricism which makes her so beautiful and exhilarating an artist." Mary Clarke said she was "at her brilliant best, dancing with the kind of happy confidence that used to infuse the work of Violette Verdy." David Dougill in *The Sunday Times* praised her "polished ease, liquid flow and musicality." Ann Nugent in *The Stage* said Evelyn Hart was "what makes the Royal Winnipeg Ballet memorable . . . She moves across the stage with effortless weightlessness to the call of the music; arms extend from her back in generous line, and movements reach their peak in high extensions . . . But above her technical gifts she has something that no teacher ever taught her, a communion with the spirit of dance." This praise echoed around Europe.

Evelyn's performances in London that year earned her a nomination, along with three other dancers, for the Society of West End Theatres Award. She didn't win it – the award went to Elisabeth Platel, from the Paris Opéra Ballet – but the nomination, and her personal triumphs throughout Europe, gave her new confidence, and confidence was something she needed in abundance. She was about to face one of the most important challenges of her career.

6 *"Canada's New Ballet Heroine"*

> Giselle *more than any other is the one ballerinas want to do. It's like the* Hamlet *of the straight theatre. You can put more into* Giselle *than you can into any other role. The Swan Queen in* Swan Lake *is fairly emotional, and* The Sleeping Beauty *is technically very demanding, but* Giselle *has a combination of everything. You have to have technique, you have to have elevation and you have to have passion; and Evelyn has all those.*
>
> – Peter Wright

*D*ancing *Giselle* was Evelyn's ambition from her earliest years as a student. When she first did the second-act pas de deux at the summer school at Banff in 1979, she felt "a sense of peace, as if I was dead – fulfilled and complete. It felt almost as if someone had blessed me on my head. I walked off and I felt as if someone had passed me into heaven."

But dancing the pas de deux in the competitions at Osaka and Varna had given her a taste of the kind of standards against which she had to measure herself and made her acutely aware of how far her interpretation had to go.

Buoyed by a record-high wave of subscribers (the 1982-83 figure of 9,403 was the largest dance subscription audience in the company's history) the RWB introduced its new production of *Giselle* in December 1982, the second full-evening classic in as many seasons.

The production chosen by Spohr was first produced by the British director and choreographer Peter Wright for the Stuttgart Ballet in 1965. Wright had subsequently mounted it for companies around the world (including the Royal Ballet and the National Ballet of Canada). The Winnipeg production was his seventeenth; each was slightly different in detail and design.

No one seriously denied that the RWB production was made possible by Evelyn's presence. It was clearly another vehicle for her talents. But Spohr was also canny enough to realize that by buying a version of a production that was

DAVID COOPER

Evelyn as the love-smitten heroine of the first act of Giselle, in an early performance of Peter Wright's new production for the RWB at the end of 1982.

widely performed abroad, he had an ideal opportunity to bring in guest artists not only for Evelyn but for other members of the company as well.

Already, for Evelyn, the ballet was bringing heady company. In November 1982 she had stopped off in Stuttgart after the European tour to work on the ballet with Richard Cragun, who was to dance it with her on tour in Canada the following spring. No sooner did she arrive home, in early December, than she was off to Grande Prairie, Alberta, to do the pas de deux with Frank Augustyn, with whom she was scheduled to dance the full *Giselle* at a National Ballet performance the next February.

In Winnipeg she also had a new partner. She had specifically asked not to be paired with Peregrine in the Winnipeg performances (she wanted someone experienced in the ballet to help her, since it was essentially her first full classical role) and the company had hired Henny Jurriens. Veronica Tennant, from the National Ballet, was flown in to dance with Peregrine.

To Peter Wright, Evelyn was something of an unknown quantity. He had seen her at the Sadler's Wells gala the previous year, and had heard wonderful reports of her, but when he first encountered her he was worried that the individuality of her manner might make it difficult for him to get her to do *Giselle* the way *he* thought it should be done, particularly since she had already worked on extracts from versions made by other choreographers. He was also bothered by the attitude of the company. Whenever Evelyn walked into the room, everything seemed to come to a halt. He felt it was not the healthiest of atmospheres for a young ballerina.

But they quickly established a strong rapport. Early in the rehearsal period he was praising her ability to understand and absorb changes very quickly, and enthusing about her astonishing musicality. As a choreographer he has always preferred to work with dancers who ask questions, even if there is sometimes disagreement, and he was particularly attracted to her eagerness to know *why* she was doing what she was doing.

Certain aspects of his production he was prepared to insist on. Some ballerinas, for instance, prefer to let their Giselles die of heartbreak or emotional torment. Wright is convinced that Giselle should be a suicide, killing herself with Albrecht's sword (a symbol of death and of the phallus). He had no problem convincing Evelyn. It was also her own vision of the role.

By no means was everything absolute seriousness. Evelyn often surprises her colleagues with her slapstick sense of humour, and "when Wright reprimanded the Wilis – a mournful band of ghosts of women who were engaged to be married but died before their wedding day – at one rehearsal for looking as if they had simply gathered to have a dainty cup of tea, she arranged for the entire corps to be photographed drinking from teacups,

DAVID COOPER

Evelyn, left in false nose and glasses, with assembled Wilis bearing teacups, in a spoof photo for Peter Wright during the Giselle *rehearsal period, 1982.*

with Evelyn herself at the front in her all-purpose false nose and spectacles. He still has the photograph. At the Christmas Eve dress rehearsal, she disappeared during one of the breaks, draped herself in garlands, stuck coloured bulbs in her ears and surprised the assembled company with an impersonation of a Christmas tree.

By showtime, however, she had everything together. Wright called her opening-night interpretation one of the most remarkable debuts in the role he could remember.

But for Evelyn, this was only the beginning of the test.

Ever since her earliest disappointments at the National Ballet School, it had been Evelyn's dream to dance with the National Ballet of Canada. In 1979, the year before she went to Varna, she actually auditioned for the company. Ballet-master David Scott conducted the audition class for artistic director Alexander Grant. Karen Kain and Nadia Potts, two of the company's leading dancers, stood at the doorway watching, curious to see what this unknown dancer from Winnipeg looked like. Their presence thoroughly intimidated her. Grant was impressed and interested, but said he didn't have a spot for her. Perhaps in a year?

By then, she was in the midst of preparations for Varna, and switching to Toronto was out of the question. But the interest on both sides remained. At a party in Toronto in the spring of 1982, she met Hazaros Surmeyan, formerly a National Ballet principal dancer and subsequently a principal character artist.

DAVID COOPER

Act One of Giselle, *with Evelyn seated on Richard Cragun's knee, and Sarah Slipper as one of her village friends; 1983.*

Surmeyan told her she should be dancing with the Toronto company, and suggested she ask Grant for an invitation. She said she couldn't possibly do that, so Surmeyan took it upon himself to do the talking. Later that evening, Grant approached her and invited her to appear with the National Ballet as a guest. He suggested *Giselle* or Frederick Ashton's version of the bucolic comedy *La Fille mal gardée*; and since Evelyn had no confidence in herself as a comedienne on the stage, *Giselle* was agreed upon.

Grant already knew her by reputation. He had seen her dance *Belong* at the National Ballet's gala in the spring of 1981, and he sensed instinctively that she was ready to tackle the classics. But he also had reasons of his own for inviting her. At that time the National Ballet had no established tradition of guest ballerinas, and Grant, looking for ways to encourage independence of thought and interpretation in a company long accustomed to being told how to crook every finger and raise every eyebrow, thought it would be useful for his dancers to work with someone from a company where individual artists were used to making their own contributions to what went on on the stage.

For Evelyn, the preparation period was a nightmare – she felt taken for granted from the start. For her first three days she didn't meet the general manager. She wasn't given the same billing as other Canadian guests. In terms of what she actually danced, she was given only minimal rehearsal time to adjust her version of the production to the version carried by the National, and when she did get rehearsal time everyone picked holes in her work: one coach told her to change her *port de bras*, another wanted different footwork, a third objected to her interpretation (which was even then, she admits, very

Russian, and quite different from the interpretation customary at the National Ballet).

A comment from a staff member about the way she was using her face was the last straw. She dashed to her dressing room and burst into tears, unable to bear the tension any longer. Moments later, she heard a knock at the door. When she opened it she found all five of the National Ballet's ballerinas: Veronica Tennant, Karen Kain, Vanessa Harwood, Mary Jago, and Nadia Potts. They crowded into the dressing room, hugging and reassuring her. "We've been going through this for years," they said. "They do it to all of us. They make you feel terrible. Don't worry, you're doing fine."

As, indeed, she was. When she did her first National Ballet *Giselle*, with Frank Augustyn as her Albrecht, at the end of February 1983, *The Globe and Mail* critic Alina Gildiner said she "stole the entire winter season." The normally reserved Toronto audience gave her a standing ovation. Evelyn returned the compliment by tossing a bouquet to the cheering crowd.

But backstage afterward, she collapsed in tears, convinced she had disgraced herself and let her host company down. Worse than that, she was terrified at having to confront all the fears she had accumulated through her past experiences in Toronto. These experiences set a pattern of expectation from her Toronto guest appearances that still has not been shaken.

Yes, says Toronto critic Michael Crabb, there were some minor disasters in that opening show. Her headdress fell off, her ribbon came undone, there was a little slip. But it didn't matter in the least. "I've never ever seen a response to the first act of *Giselle* as there was to Evelyn that night, ever, anywhere," he says. "She just blew the house away. There were sobs all over the theatre. There were grown men coming out with tears down their cheeks. It was wonderful."

Anna Kisselgoff, who had been flown in by the *New York Times*, led off her review with the declaration that "Canadian ballet has a new heroine." The performance, she said, "thrusts her into the first ranks of North America's new generation of rising stars."

Part of what makes Peter Wright's version of *Giselle* so appealing is his determination to stick to logical plot-progression within the Romantic ballet conventions – a kind of modernized naturalism that makes the work more acceptable to a modern public. It is an approach that meshes naturally with Evelyn's taste for the emotional and the theatrical dimensions of dance. While she fully understood the technical demands of the role, and the weight of public expectation created by the *Giselle* performance tradition, she was convinced that it was as important to convey the full emotional texture of the piece as to get all the technical trickery right. Working on *Romeo and Juliet* had taught her that standing still was sometimes as significant as moving.

From the start, her interpretation of the character was highly individualistic. The poet and critic who wrote the ballet's scenario, Théophile Gautier, said the original Giselle, Carlotta Grisi, was "nature and artlessness personified" and praised her "perfection, lightness, boldness, chaste and refined seductiveness." But in Evelyn's interpetation of Wright's updated version (in which a country girl falls in love with a wayward prince, finds herself betrayed by him and, in an agony of love and madness, kills herself), the first act presented a Giselle who was no rustic innocent but a girl with a sly eye for romantic excitement, acting on impulse from a bold heart – artless, perhaps, but anything but demure. The interpretation heightened the pathos of the mad scene and her death, and established a fine contrast for the exquisitely attenuated Romantic yearnings that she brought to the ethereal second act, in which the spirit of Giselle (now one of the Wilis) saves her betrayer from being danced to death by the band of ghosts.

It was an interpretation that communicated. When she performed *Giselle* with Richard Cragun in Vancouver in March that year, Susan Mertens, dance critic for *The Vancouver Sun*, said she danced "with a simplicity and an emotional openness that are deeply affecting. Her first act – her shining-eyed delight in loving and being loved, the exquisite pathos of her gentle madness – goes directly to the heart. Her second act – dancing as if she had contrived to transfigure bone and sinew into pure, animated spirit – is on an altogether different plane."

Giselle was not, however, the only role Evelyn danced that spring and early summer. Despite her reluctance to accept Peregrine as a partner, she found herself dancing with him in *Belong* frequently during the company's U.S. and Canadian tour, and in *Romeo and Juliet* at home, on tour, and in the CBC's television studios.

And again, she found time for comedy. During rehearsals for the television taping of *Romeo and Juliet* in Toronto, she and the CBC technicians had a running battle to see who could get the most laughs. As she was being carried through Verona in a covered litter, for instance, she parted the curtains and stuck out her head . . . wearing goggle-eye sunglasses. When the crew complained they weren't getting enough credit, she turned up on the set with a sign saying Face by Daisy, Hair by Anita. In the balcony scene, she used binoculars to scan the garden for Romeo. She blacked out her teeth for the death scene. Between *fouettés*, she blew a party whistle. The technicians responded by putting a hot-water bottle beneath her as she lay on her slab in the tomb scene – and a props man replaced Juliet's sleeping potion with a container of smoking dry ice and two straws.

Toronto was also a stop on the RWB's *Romeo and Juliet* performance tour. The National Ballet's version of *Romeo and Juliet* is by John Cranko, and quite different from the version by van Dantzig. As William Littler pointed out in *The Toronto Star*, van Dantzig's version doesn't have Cranko's gift of movement invention or his ability to move with the lyrical flow of Prokofiev's music. But it compensates for that by its surging energy, its passionate impulse, and its strong dramatic characterization. The sense of isolation that van Dantzig creates for Juliet, said Littler, "plays to Hart's ability to give a nervous intensity to her dancing, to stretch herself physically to the point of danger . . . It is a case of mating a great talent to a great role."

Even so, taking van Dantzig's *Romeo and Juliet* to the home city of the National Ballet was audacious, particularly since the visit marked the first time any Canadian company had ventured into Toronto with a full-length classic. But it paid off. Again, the Toronto audience leaped to its feet. Alina Gildiner in *The Globe and Mail* called Evelyn "superlative . . . It is easy to see why she has her reputation for greatness." In *The Toronto Star* Michael Crabb called her "an ideal Juliet" and analyzed "the irresistible magic she works on audiences."

"Despite the actual strength of her dancing," he wrote, "there is an inherent frailty and vulnerability about Hart's stage personality. In part this is communicated through movement . . . [She] has a rare gift for arresting the flow of a sequence of steps, for changing their speed and direction, in a way that intensifies one's sense of her almost hyper-nervous energy. Hart has also learned to use her expressive face to advantage. She can convey a world of meaning with one telling glance, and her finely-detailed gestures appear consistently natural and spontaneous."

Veronica Tennant, by now a firm friend, sent Evelyn a note after the RWB's opening saying: "Thanks for the inspiration you have given me." For the audiences, too, Evelyn was becoming a favourite. The wife of federal cabinet minister Alistair Gillespie caused a stir in the lobby of the Toronto theatre when she discovered she had tickets for a night when Evelyn was not scheduled to dance and demanded new tickets in a good location for one of Evelyn's performances.

For Evelyn, it all meant she was finally beginning to find her footing as an artist after all the pressures of being a gold medallist. The big roles were giving her a chance, she said that summer, to relax and gain confidence. Because as she learned them, working toward a goal of interpretation and performance, she was able to feel like a student again, able to hide behind the work, to lose herself in the process.

Not that she had much time to hide. Chuck Marahrens kept her on the move through the summer and early fall. Early in August she danced the *Giselle* act two pas de deux with another Marahrens client, American Ballet Theatre's Patrick Bissell, and the balcony pas de deux from van Dantzig's *Romeo and Juliet* with Henny Jurriens at an open-air gala at New York's Liberty State Park. Clive Barnes in the *New York Post* called her "a natural Giselle with a lightness and delicacy to the manner born." She repeated the role opposite Jurriens (also partnering him in the Black Swan pas de deux) on a similar bill at the venerable Jacob's Pillow dance festival in Massachusetts the following week.

In October and early November she was back in Japan, dancing the lead in *Giselle* in Tokyo and Osaka with the Homura Tomoi company. Between those dates she also managed to slip away for a late-October gala performance in Munich to raise funds for the Heinz Bösl Foundation, a charity that supports a school for young dancers. Dancing act two of *Giselle* opposite Richard Cragun, she found herself the hit of the show. The critics tripped over themselves to spill praise.

"She feels the music, and when she dances she seems to forget everything she learned before," said the reviewer for the *Münchner Merkur*. "She is the paragon of the Romantic ballerina, and her dancing transcends time and space."

"As transparent as a creature from another world, floating over the stage, displaying the most difficult technique in a pure and noble way . . . you would search for a very long time to find a Giselle like this," said another reviewer.

"Who didn't get goosebumps?" asked a third.

Evelyn, meanwhile, was getting goosebumps of her own. On the schedule for the New Year was her London debut in *Giselle* – at the direct invitation of the man who had made the RWB's production, Peter Wright.

Somehow, in all that travelling that fall, she managed to fit in an October trip to Ottawa for her investiture as an Officer of the Order of Canada, the second of three levels attainable in the country's highest civil award. The recognition thrilled her. She felt honoured to have her contribution to Canada's image recognized, and to be numbered among a group that included such celebrated artists as the contralto Maureen Forrester.

She invited David Moroni to escort her to the ceremony. He was, after all, the man who had been most influential in the development of her talent; he had guided and advised her, calmed and comforted her. She was especially moved, still, by the poignancy of dancing with him in *Nutcracker* – she as Louise, the glamorous ballerina from the state theatre, he as Drosselmeier, the imperious ballet-master. When they danced together, it was, she said, almost true to life in its renewal of their pupil-teacher relationship.

At the investiture ceremony at Rideau Hall, she was far more nervous than when she was on stage, principally because she was afraid she would trip on the skirt of her long, jewelled, black gown. In fact, the gown came close to embarrassing her all by itself. When Governor-General Ed Schreyer pinned the medal to her chiffon-and-jersey neckline, the medal's weight pulled the top of the dress open and down – "so here I am, feeling very risqué, walking back, trying to haul the medal up. It was potentially a real disappointment for the crowd: ballerina boobs."

Peter Wright's invitation to Evelyn to dance *Giselle* with the Sadler's Wells Royal Ballet in January 1984 was a direct result of his pleasure with her handling of the role when he mounted the ballet in Winnipeg.

She performed it twice in London, England, opposite David Ashmole, and while not every reviewer was enthusiastic, those who were wrote more raves for her growing portfolio. Clement Crisp, in the *Financial Times*, spoke of a performance of "extreme distinction, a born Giselle whose interpretation is clear in focus, luminous in its Romantic sensibility and unerring in taste." He called her "a new and outstanding heroine" and a "true and compelling"

DAVID COOPER

Curtain-call for Giselle.

Giselle. Mary Clarke in *The Guardian* said Evelyn's performances established her as "a Romantic ballerina of rare quality." Clarke compared Evelyn's first-act characterizations to the portrayal made famous by Ulanova; the mad scene, she said, "must be among the great ones." And she suggested, as Alexander Grant already had, that Evelyn would make an ideal Lise in *La Fille mal gardée*.

Clarke also praised Wright for his "happy and generous" invitation to Evelyn to appear with the company and called for her return, arguing that she would inspire the younger dancers in the company and challenge the more senior. "Her style is different yet it sits most easily within the framework of the SWRB," she wrote. "She dances as a member of the company, not as an exotic, albeit as a most precious, guest."

Wright plainly agreed. He invited Evelyn back for a three-month spell the following fall, dancing the two principal classical roles she had so far never tackled: the Swan Queen in *Swan Lake*, and Aurora in *The Sleeping Beauty*.

Before she left for home from that initial engagement, she also danced in Kenneth MacMillan's ragtime-based *Elite Syncopations*. She learned it in six one-hour rehearsals and did her first full run-through on the stage, at an open-to-the-public dress rehearsal. She was just about to start her solo when someone asked her where her cane was. "Cane?" she asked. "*Cane?*" "The cane you twirl like a baton during your solo," she was told. "Did no one mention it?" She went on without it.

In attendance at her opening performance was the choreographer himself, accompanied by Alexander Grant and Michael Crabb. MacMillan watched her performance of his work for a while, then turned to his companions and said, "I haven't seen that before, but I think I like it."

Much of the period between her January 1984 appearances in London and her return to the Sadler's Wells Royal Ballet as a resident guest in the fall was occupied by *Giselle*.

In late February and early March she danced four performances with Roland Petit's Ballet de Marseille. Scared to go abroad by herself, she took Chuck Marahrens along as company and chaperone and found herself treated like a big star. It made her nervous. She felt she was operating under false pretences.

It was in Marseille she danced for the first time with Jean Charles Gil, the company's twenty-four-year-old principal male. She was both entranced and intrigued. With the David Peregrine connection finally broken (he had left in January for a four-month guest spell with the San Francisco Ballet) the question of finding a new partner was high on Evelyn's list of priorities. Gil danced with passion and partnered her superbly. Might *he* possibly be the partner she had been looking for for so long?

In April the RWB, swallowing nervously, took *Giselle* to New York's Brooklyn Academy of Music. Although Evelyn was by now no stranger to the New York critics, this was officially her New York debut – "the crucial test," according to Arnold Spohr. Her performances won widespread praise, though the company fared less well. New York's *Newsday*, for example, called her a "world-class dancer . . . in a company that is only fair." Later the same month, she danced *Giselle* twice more with the National Ballet in Toronto during a two-week guest run.

This was clearly a *Giselle* of considerable staying power, and Anna Kisselgoff put her finger on the reason for that in her review of the BAM appearances in the *New York Times*. "Every so often," she said, "a dancer emerges who . . . communicates a magic that many a more 'correct' dancer cannot."

The lack of "correctness" that was at the heart of Evelyn's early troubles with the National Ballet of Canada was now the root of her interpretation's appeal. Few of the great dancers have textbook-pure classical technique, and Evelyn was quicker than anyone to recognize and acknowledge her technical deficiencies. On a good day, if she was feeling good or the music was working for her, she could pull off a reasonable technique, but at the Munich gala the previous fall she had stood in the wings and wept as she watched the young Katherine Healy perform all kinds of technical impossibilities.

Technique, however, was not what people watched Evelyn for. Her forte was emotional expression and a lyricism rooted deeply in her own romantic-spiritual worldview. And now, for the first time, her encounters with the classics were allowing her to shade in her own way stories that dealt with love, that touched the human spirit. The modernistic Juliet of van Dantzig had been a start. But it was the intrinsically Romantic *Giselle* that first allowed those impulses full free rein.

She had known instinctively since her earliest years as a dancer that it would. It was while she was dancing the *Giselle* pas de deux in public for the first time, opposite André Lewis in a gymnasium at the University of Manitoba in 1979, that she first felt what she calls the "spirituality" of her dancing – her ability to make a connection with an audience and hold it spellbound. It felt like an overflow of emotion inside her; her heart was in her throat.

She had never been that deeply moved within herself by her own dancing before, but the sensation has recurred frequently since, most often in performances of *Giselle*. It usually happens when she feels at her most creative and most untrammelled by demands, freed by her confidence in herself and her partner to abandon herself into the role.

She has also been able to experience it as a recipient. Watching Marcia Haydée at the Alberta Ballet gala was one such occasion. Watching the Royal Ballet's Anthony Dowell rehearsing in Miami when they danced there together in the summer of 1982 was another. "I was standing behind him; he wasn't rehearsing anything significant. But I had this awesome, overwhelming feeling that this was God. What was going through my head was a picture of the broadest plain and a sky opening up with this incredible light."

Given her background, the spiritual connection is probably inevitable, though in interviews she has always hesitated to talk about God. It scares people off. But she says, "I don't know any other concept that is great enough to cover that kind of feeling. It's as if you feel your soul is going to burst, as if this little frame cannot contain, cannot conceive the depth and intensity of feeling it gives you inside yourself."

What she is talking about is an elevation, through a performance, to "a state that we're maybe not familiar with. It's as if that person is merely the vehicle for something greater. It's a level of absolute purity. Maybe this is what Pavlova meant when she said it was our duty to develop absolute beauty in our lives and eliminate everything other, tangible or intangible, thought and deed, and not be dragged down by the pettiness of human nature."

It is at these moments, she believes, that the individual transcends the self and contact is made with the human core.

With *Giselle* confidently tucked under her belt, it naturally followed that she would want to tackle the other two classical yardsticks, the Swan Queen in *Swan Lake* and Aurora in *The Sleeping Beauty*.

During her two-week stay in Toronto in the spring of 1984, she had made her first attempt at Aurora with the National Ballet of Canada. Though she looked back on it later as one of her happiest performances, the experience was another logistical disaster. No one had time to teach her the role properly. She had six days of scattered rehearsal and was still learning it hours before she went on stage. For the first time in her career, she found herself faking things in performance.

The fakery was good enough to win two curtain-calls within the first act. *The Globe and Mail* critic Alina Gildiner said Evelyn imbued the role with the kind of unaccustomed drama that gave it an altogether new resonance. Again, it was a matter of Evelyn allowing herself to run with a romantic notion. Whenever she had seen *The Sleeping Beauty* as an audience member, it had nearly bored her to sleep. She had vowed that she would approach it differently – give it drama, create a story. Opposite Raymond Smith (another

Carter school graduate) she made the first-act princess a dreamy, romantic innocent, so that by the time the later acts came around, she had strongly established a character to play against. The story became meaningful; emotion was communicated.

In July 1984 she travelled with the RWB to the Olympic Arts Festival in Los Angeles, dancing among other things the *Giselle* pas de deux with guest artist Frank Augustyn, but staying well clear of Peregrine, who had rejoined the Winnipeg troupe after his guest spell with the San Francisco Ballet. And then, exhausted by the stresses of the season just finished, and suffering a stress fracture in an ankle, she took a rare month-long holiday, even turning down an invitation to dinner with the Queen in London in order to be alone. The invitation was "a great honour," she said, "but when you're in the desert and someone offers you a million dollars when all you really want is a glass of water . . . At this point I do have to take care of my physical needs as well." She took care of these needs with a simple regimen of complete rest, staying at home for the duration of her holiday and luxuriating in her temporary freedom from responsibility.

Spiritually and physically refreshed, the ankle repaired, she joined the company on tour in September in Greece (dancing *Romeo and Juliet* with Henny Jurriens) and Egypt, then flew to London to begin a three-month engagement with the Sadler's Wells company.

On paper, this engagement was exactly what Evelyn needed. Peter Wright was offering her the chance to get *Swan Lake* and *The Sleeping Beauty* solidly into her muscles, performing them on tour in places where there was no pressure to *be* Evelyn Hart, with all the medal-winning glamour that that implied, since no one in Britain – outside London – knew who Evelyn Hart was.

Once again she found herself facing an abrupt and brutal demonstration of the facts of life in the unprotected world outside Winnipeg. Since there had been no one in Winnipeg who knew enough about *Swan Lake* to be able to coach her in the role, she was forced to learn it in a week on the road with the SWRB, and she made her debut as the Swan Queen at an hour's notice in a tent beneath pouring skies in the university city of Cambridge.

Despite all that, or perhaps because of it, she scored another triumph. Critic Clement Crisp, by now something of a Hart groupie, was present for her debut and was in no doubt about her achievement.

"To find in a débutante Odette-Odile the true stuff of the role, set out in terms of physical and temperamental refinement, is rare indeed," he wrote in the *Financial Times*. "Miss Hart brings to the part a fine-boned and expansive technique – line pure, open; technique secure, fluent – and a dramatic sensibility that tell of her entire right to the ballet.

"But more than this . . . there is the indefinable and unassailable fact of her authority as a ballerina."

The problems began when she repeated the role at Covent Garden. Covent Garden, home of the Royal Ballet, is the heart and shrine of ballet in Britain, and certain expectations are placed on artists who perform there. Yet Evelyn's experience of the world of ballet had been so sheltered that she had only seen one live *Swan Lake* in her life before she began to learn it, and when she made her Covent Garden debut in the role, it was only the third time she had performed it. In performance, moreover, she missed six of the thirty-two *fouettés* that have become virtually obligatory in the Black Swan pas de deux.

The audience was enthusiastic. Spohr loved her performance, and so did Rudi van Dantzig, who had flown in to see her. But the reviews (there were sixteen) were predominantly cool, and although she was assured later that the response was primarily political (how dare "a little person from a little wee company that they've never heard of come into Covent Garden"), she took it hard.

Then came *The Sleeping Beauty*, and again, despite the admiration Peter Wright had expressed in Winnipeg for her openness and her argumentative spirit, she had a miserable time over interpretation. Nothing she did seemed right – arms, face, feet – nothing. Whenever she tried to introduce her own interpretation, she was told that wasn't the way it was done. She says she didn't begin to win approval for what she was doing until she had started to become "a little Margot Fonteyn clone."

She also had too little to do. The touring schedule might call for four performances of *The Sleeping Beauty* in a week, along with other programming. She would get one of the performances, Henny Jurriens (who was partnering her) would come over from Amsterdam on, say, the Wednesday for a Thursday performance, and then for the rest of the week she'd be left twiddling her thumbs, without performance or rehearsal. She wasn't used to being underworked, and the empty days made her miserable.

Wright doesn't deny that her time with the company was "very hard for her . . . She wasn't used to our way of working at all, which is very tough when we're out on the road – not much time to rehearse and not much time to perfect things. You just get on and do it, and she found that very hard. We weren't able to offer the continuity of rehearsal that they could give her always in Winnipeg, and she found that very frustrating. She was also their prima ballerina, and that wasn't the case with us, we had a lot of other top principal dancers." As a stranger in the company, she was also often lonely, and Wright, much as he might have wished to be able to give her more attention than he did, was fully occupied as company head.

There have since been suggestions that she had been "mollycoddled" by Spohr and his associates too much, to the extent that her demands for full rehearsals with SWRB might have been unreasonable. On the other hand, this *was* the first time she danced *The Sleeping Beauty*, and if ever there's a time when a ballerina needs a full-time nursemaid, her first Aurora is it.

At one point Evelyn went to Wright and told him she couldn't take it any longer and wanted out of her contract. He was able to calm her down and she lasted the full twelve weeks. In retrospect, his view is that she did some wonderful performances with SWRB and had a great personal success. But at the time Evelyn was convinced it had been a failure of catastrophic proportions. She had gone to London in the hope that her appearances in those roles would advance her career. If anything, she felt, the adventure had set her career several steps back.

She became convinced, as the years passed and no more invitations from Wright came her way, that she had ruined her chances in London forever – by "freaking out" on stage and not finishing her *fouettés*, by making trouble about partners, by being difficult over interpretations, by generally earning a reputation as a problem for the company. It was not a happy episode.

7 "Me? A Ballerina?"

*T*he sources of the self-doubt that made Evelyn Hart's time at Sadler's Wells so distressing can be found in her childhood, but they had been reinforced right through her life.

She has struggled throughout her career against a sense of personal inadequacy. As a young dancer she often wouldn't go to parties or receptions because she didn't have the right thing to wear – and didn't trust her taste to tell her what the right thing was.

Humility was something that was drilled into her from her earliest years. Just because she had been blessed by God with a talent, her father used to tell her, that didn't mean that she was better than anyone else. When she went home to her family, bubbling with the excitement of her first solo with the RWB, she picked up a sense of disapproval – isn't our Ev getting a bit too big for her boots?

It all made for immense conflicts within her. Shaped by her upbringing, she couldn't fully believe that she danced well, yet that was her dream. To have a career like Makarova's was her life's ambition.

Initially, the contradiction within her wasn't anything she was prepared to recognize. She rationalized her lack of belief in her work by telling herself that she could never come close to the dancing of people she really admired. When she went to Odessa, the dancers thanked her for showing them, finally, how to do *Giselle*. Embarrassed, she protested she was only a beginner. When people

DAVID COOPER

Evelyn as Giselle, with Henny Jurriens as Albrecht.

hailed her as the toast of the town, she compared herself with her mental images of the world's top dancers and asked herself what on earth they were talking about: her body was wrong, her face was wrong, nothing was right.

What she considers her lack of good looks torments her. She has always felt like a Plain Jane. Her face seems like a blob to her. Her eyes (a cornflower blue) are too small. Her ears are too big. Her lips are non-existent (she calls herself "the lipless wonder" – once, in rehearsal, Arnold Spohr told her to relax the tension in her lips and not make them so tight, and she had to tell him they *were* relaxed; eventually, she says, she'll get a silicone job on her lips to fill them out). Her natural hair is a mousy brown, so she dyes it.

"It's pretty hard to look a man lovingly in the eyes," she says, "because I cannot imagine having to look back at my face." When she first danced with Rex Harrington she toyed with the idea of giving him a photo of Audrey Hepburn and telling him to visualize the actress in her place, "because I get a beautiful face to look at and he doesn't. But you have to come to terms with the fact that you're not going to win Miss Teen Canada." Her own suggested title for this book was "Me? A ballerina?"

Her mental image of the perfect ballerina made her feel like a usurper. Her earliest experiences persuaded her that she didn't possess the instrument to be a world-class dancer, and it is a conviction she retains. She looks in the mirror and she sees prominent shoulderblades, a bum that sticks out, funny-shaped legs, short feet, a plain face. So when she sees someone with more acceptable attributes – a better-shaped body, or better turn-out – she feels inadequate. She can't allow herself to believe that she can be as good, that she fits into the ballet mould. No matter how hard she tries, she still feels like that insecure little girl from Dorchester, Ontario, knocking on the doors of the National Ballet School.

At the same time, she wanted it all, and wanted it with a passion. What was the point of working if it wasn't for a reason? So she drove herself harder and harder. There were times when even Evelyn would sneak a secret look at tapes of herself in performance – *Giselle* in Tokyo in 1988, for instance – and would have to admit that she really wasn't so bad. The trouble was, she couldn't let herself feel special, because while success was closer to her heart than anything else in the world, it also wasn't allowed.

So the closer she came to her goal, the further ahead she moved the goalposts.

Though unwilling to believe praise, she is even more vulnerable to negative criticism. When critic Anita Finkel demolished her performance in *Giselle* in a long review in *Dance Magazine* in 1984, Evelyn was so distraught that for weeks she was frightened to set foot on the stage, and she carried the hurt inside her for years. David Y. H. Lui recalls an emotional outburst in the wardrobe room before a 1987 gala he organized for Ballet B.C. "She was sure she was going to be the flop of the program. As it turned out she was sandwiched between Irina Kolpakova and Natalia Makarova, which I suppose is not a very comfortable place for anybody, but I told her, look, if anybody can pull this off it's going to be you, and of course she did. She was the hit of the night."

When Chuck Marahrens arranged for her to get an audition with Mikhail Baryshnikov for American Ballet Theatre, she refused to go, partly because she felt auditioning was beneath her dignity at that stage of her career, but mostly because of her fear that she might actually be rejected. Even if she were to accept her gift, what guarantee did she have that the well would not run dry? Not accepting it was a way to protect herself against losing it.

Other dancers, too, threatened her terribly. She found it easy to believe almost anyone was better – and if they were, why should they not take her place, or equally unacceptable, exist alongside her as an equal?

Her insecurity was part of what helped her communicate so strongly on the stage. Dancers who are too confident and comfortable in their roles can be uninspiring to watch. A hint of vulnerability, of a slight nervousness, can lift a performance for an audience. A lack of confidence can also help the artist develop. Dancers who are satisfied with themselves are rarely the great ones; it is the never-ending push for perfection that gives the best their edge.

Part of Evelyn's problem with perfectionism lies in her attitude to work, and in that respect her experiences in Europe and with Henny Jurriens were revealing. Evelyn has always regarded rehearsal like performance; she wants to get everything right immediately (perhaps a hangover from her days at the National Ballet School, where standards were routinely so high that you didn't dare fall over). But Jurriens always used to tell her not to get frustrated if something didn't go as planned in rehearsal; that was what work was about. She saw the same thing when she was in France. If something didn't work the dancers just laughed and tried it again. No one lost any self-esteem or standing with their colleagues.

More frequent, though, have been the times when her confidence has been at ground zero, and she needs love and attention to get on the stage. "She is on a tightrope; she is on the borderline of greatness, and all her nerve-ends, every pore in her being, is alive for the spark of release," says Arnold Spohr. "Once she's on-stage, she's in her land of performance, ruling and conquering for that evening. But the next day it starts all over again, and she has to find that same element of release, and it doesn't always come. That's why it's so important for her to find the base you get from rehearsal that will carry her through to that night until the great powers are with her again. She goes through this terrified state, insanity nearly, until she's on, and away she goes to rule that night – but it has to be. It's not only the fear of technique, but also the fear of whether she can find all those intangibles of love and hate and bring them to reality. The technical things you can master. But what you can't master is the intangibles. It's the unknown that's so terrifying."

It takes just one thing to ruin a show for Evelyn. There's a part in *Nuages* right at the beginning, a pirouette that she does by herself, and as soon as that's over she feels home free. I have seen her in tears in her dressing room after performances that have been positively incandescent, simply because she feels she has done less than her best. The incident is usually something the average audience-member wouldn't notice – perhaps she has fallen off pointe or missed a lift – but for Evelyn it is enough to destroy any pleasure she might have had from the evening.

Veronica Tennant thinks Evelyn's self-denigration, her self-punishment, was perhaps necessary for the creation of that artistry. Maybe, she speculates, she *had* to go through all that agony to create what she did.

Evelyn measures herself against the achievements of others constantly, and applies the same high standards to what she sees. "She puts people on a pedestal, and then she gets terribly disappointed when she finds that she is so much higher than them," Henny Jurriens once said. Certainly, when you press her to define a ballerina she would be satisfied with, she mentions technical phenomena like Sylvie Guillem, Gelsey Kirkland, and, of course, Makarova. Then she adds: "But they don't really touch me – not like Marcia [Haydée]."

If you go on to press her to name the ballerina she most identifies with as a performer, it is Anna Pavlova – "not the dancer," as Serge Lifar said about Pavlova, "but the *genius* of the dance."

When she first went into psychotherapy, Evelyn worried about what the effects might be. What would she do if she discovered that deep down she didn't love dance? (In fact, what she found over the years was that it helped her love dance more, not less.)

Others worried that if she became straightened out, she would lose the edge of insecurity and rawness that gave her work on the stage such impact. It was a concern she shared. But Arnold Spohr believes that it would be impossible to straighten her out even if anyone wanted to, because the source of her artistry lies "in every part of her being, where no one will ever be able to tread, because it is not in our capacity. This great, emotional, disturbing thing that happens when she dances . . . there are some things that you just can't put into words – you just feel it, like love. You can't see what dimension it is, it just is there. God is the muse, I guess, and no one can pinpoint what made it, including the ballerina."

Richard Cragun thinks "a certain kind of fragility – a walking along the tightrope – was always there." But he also makes the point that she was "born into a generation that needs other people to help straighten their lives out." While he believes "there is a survival instinct in her that is going to come to her aid very well" he wonders whether she might be one of "the generation of Western dancers who secretly lament the fact that they haven't had a tragedy in their life – escaping from Russia, for instance, or a world war kind of drama."

These are people, he believes, who are "subconsciously looking for a difficult wall to break through in life, and this wall has become her mind, something to fight against, part and parcel of what she is about." He draws parallels with the way we have tended to romanticize the Russian ballerina Olga Spessivtseva, who ended up in a mental institution, or Gelsey Kirkland, who took illegal drugs and went through a mental collapse.

"It's dramatic, it's alive," he says, "it's not just a girl washing her morning dishes and going in doing a *plié*, heaven forbid. It's 'I'm going to a psychiatrist five times a week, I must be pretty kooky, I'm all right.' I can relate to that very well. But it's not that we think we're crazy. And we certainly don't want to be told, listen, we can straighten you out, because we don't want to be straightened out."

He found when she danced with him in Stuttgart that he was in one sense treating her like a kid sister – a common response to her basic emotional neediness – but in another sense was also finding himself drawn into an emotional involvement. "I think you make love on stage every time you go out, whether it's an abstract ballet or *Giselle*," he says, "and the fact that it's platonic is a safeguard against complications. You can't sleep with every partner you dance with . . . but if it is hanging in the air it can be very beautiful. And that unspoken who-are-you, what-are-we-all-about, touching-the-hand, what-does-it-all-mean is something Evelyn relates to very strongly."

He adds, though, that her lack of confidence can also be downright irritating. He remembers being with her for a series of gala performances in Japan in the summer of 1988. They would line up for the bows, "and if you were in front of her, she'd be going, 'Oh, my God, I can't go on behind you,' or if she was in front of us, 'How can I go on in front of you?' For five minutes it was funny, and then for the rest of the time it was a downer."

What made it irritating was his perception that she is not "the little moun-tain flower of Canada" that many perceive, but a manipulative woman trying to get everyone to agree with the world that she wants to create. In that, he believes, she is keeping company with all the great manipulators of ballet – "Plisetskaya, Fonteyn, Fracci, Haydée, Alonso: these are your *ballerinas*, but I say that lovingly, because, God love 'em, that's the way they have to be, and they wouldn't be what they are if they weren't. Strangely enough they all have a wonderful feminine childish personality – but in the studio they have steel, and they need it to survive."

Henny Jurriens agreed. Half of her won't accept her talents, he said, "but the other half of her knows damn, damn well." Even so, says David Y. H. Lui, while there is no doubt that Evelyn wants to be fussed over, she doesn't do it deliberately. She's not conniving, he says. She does it because she genuinely needs something.

What she needs, says Cragun, is "the strong person who doesn't agree with her to keep her on track – the strong father, the strong lover, the strong man, but she still wants to be the absolutely independent woman. The question is, how much of it is necessary, how much should be tampered with, and how much should be left alone? That's the riddle."

Henny Jurriens was that strong person. Their partnership seemed blessed from its first days in Amsterdam, though Jurriens was never under any delusions about the difficulty of making it work. Despite the fact that he always found her generous and giving as a partner, her talent was initially a frustration.

"I considered myself an extremely creative person," he said, "but I suddenly discovered that there are different levels of creativity. I also considered myself extremely musical, and then you discover that there is a person who can divide a bar of music not only into three or six but into 150. You get frustrated, because first you can't hear it and you don't understand it, and then at some point when you do hear it you discover that she is right. And that in the beginning was very frustrating. You have to accept that you always can learn. Evelyn insists on certain things, and you think that she's wrong, but once you start doing it you see that she's right. You learn very fast, and then you suddenly discover that she accepts a lot of your suggestions too – although she would not always admit that. She would say, 'No, I don't want to do that,' but then at the next rehearsal she would make it her own discovery, which I never mind. Then you get to another stage where you really get to know each other and can feel her weaknesses and her strengths – like a marriage. And then you really start to create together."

In his partnership with Evelyn, his generosity of spirit allowed him to push his own needs as an artist into second place. At the beginning he saw his role as simply providing support for her and showing her in the best possible light. His career was approaching its end, and he felt fortunate to be working with such a dancer. Later, he came to realize the fallacy of that thinking. It wasn't good enough just to be a prop behind her – he was short-changing himself as an artist, and probably short-changing the partnership as well. Prodded by choreographer-director Benjamin Harkarvy, who saw them dance together at the Jacob's Pillow dance festival and who recognized precisely what Jurriens was doing to guide Evelyn toward individual stardom, he spent the balance of his career – about two seasons – working on himself, working on his variations, polishing his technique, asserting his own individuality. He began to use her talents to raise the level of his own, and in the end the all-important sense of the performing individual came through. It made her feel, she says, "very secure and comfortable and sometimes very inspired – very proud of him, very happy to be able to dance with him."

When Jurriens decided to give up dancing, Evelyn saw the decision as a personal disaster for herself. They had reached a point of such remarkable mutuality on the stage that they were able to insert new subtleties of interpretation quite spontaneously – subtleties so small that audiences might miss them entirely but which would glow with meaning for the dancers.

Her relationship with her family, meanwhile, had remained estranged. Once she had reached Winnipeg, she left her family behind, though Elly remembers a glorious week one summer when the two of them took a holiday at home going through their old dolls and clothes together, and in 1979 Evelyn went to Mitchell to bake a cake (cake-decorating was one of her favourite hobbies as a child) for her grandmother's eighty-first birthday. But one by one, her siblings were married – one by one, she missed the weddings.

Judy was first, in the summer of 1976. She married precisely at the time Evelyn entered the RWB. Evelyn was going to be a bridesmaid; dresses had been made. But an air strike meant she would have had to go by train and miss a day of rehearsal, and Evelyn, just six days into the company, backed out.

In 1983, it was Elly's turn. Again, it was a difficult time for Evelyn, who had only limited time available to work with visiting choreographers. But Evelyn promised to be there "with bells on" if they'd hold the wedding on a weekend. As it turned out they couldn't, so once again, Evelyn was missing. Maxine brought along a stuffed ballerina doll instead – more than a mere joke, thinks John Hart.

COURTESY EVELYN HART

Sister Elly's 1983 wedding, minus Evelyn. From left: Maxine; brother, John; Elly's husband, Glenn Buckmaster; Elly (holding the stuffed doll Maxine brought as a substitute for Evelyn); Sandy Stuart (Judy's husband); and sister Judy, holding her son, Luke.

John's own wedding took place the following year, and by that time, no one even expected her to be there. They simply called her and told her it was going to happen. Once again, the doll stood in for Evelyn in the wedding photos. Elly jokes that when Evelyn gets married, the entire family will boycott the event and send a group photograph instead.

Maxine, to whom the integrity of the family unit is of particular importance, always worried that the prolonged periods when Evelyn made no contact were the times when she most needed the family support. She would have been happy to help, but she felt she should wait to be asked rather than push herself forward. Now she regrets deeply that she left Evelyn alone to struggle. "She didn't have enough warm clothes; she literally suffered it through," says Maxine. "But then I think we all felt that way. That is our Protestant ethic, that it was good to feel that we were suffering."

Evelyn recognized her mother's burning need to be part of her life, but whenever she did attempt to involve her, it ended in disaster. She would invite her to Winnipeg, but then she would never have time to be with her, and Maxine would stay by herself at the apartment, ironing and cleaning, upset at being left alone.

"For artistry to exist, and mastery and perfection, it requires that kind of concentration, so you don't want to stand in the way of that," says Judy. "But at the same time as a family member you require certain input. It's a hard thing to balance: to decide whether it's better just to be mad or forget about her, or to do what you can to encourage her. It's like a picture cut out of the family portrait."

When Evelyn was first in the company, she didn't even have the confidence to ask the management for tickets for them. Judy went through a period when she felt very hurt that her three children seemed to hold no interest for Evelyn.

As a twin, Elly finds the lack of sustained emotional response particularly hard. She recognizes that Evelyn is so deeply involved in dance that she will naturally tend to choose as friends people from the dance world who can be more understanding and supportive about the artistic aspects of her life. She mentions an Ottawa dance teacher, Linda Jamieson, whom Evelyn counts as one of her closest friends. But while Elly understands the dance connection, she admits that she "gets kind of hurt sometimes" when Evelyn opts to spend free time on Ottawa performance visits with Linda rather than with her.

She also finds it disconcerting to be the sister of such a high-profile individual. Reporting for work at a new job, she was discouraged to find that the only thing her new colleagues wanted to hear about was Evelyn. At a function organized by her canoe club, she "made the mistake" of wearing an RWB T-shirt, and was deluged by fellow-members wanting to know about her sister.

Still, she always makes sure she's present whenever the company performs in Ottawa. It's a part of her sister's life she doesn't feel she can afford to miss. Often, she sits in the audience with tears rolling down her face, unable to believe that she is looking at her twin.

But ultimately, the family is proud of what Evelyn has achieved, and recognizes the pressures under which she has had to work. John remembers fondly the first time he saw her on a national television talk-show, "Canada AM." What he saw was a suave and sophisticated woman in a high-fashion dress, answering difficult questions in a refined and easy manner. "I said, '*That*? That's my sister? That's the little waif I used to throw around the backyard?'"

Her rapport with her siblings remains deep, despite the physical separation. When John called her to tell her he had named his first-born after their father, they both wept. A keen amateur musician, he belonged to a vocal group that performed funny songs about lawyers and judges at lawyers' conventions, and he was thrilled when in 1986 Evelyn made time in Toronto to go to watch *him* perform.

Whenever the family members do get together with Evelyn, in whatever configuration, it's as if she had never been away. "We'll complain about Ev behind her back," says Judy, "but as soon as she's there we're there, and we have wonderful times."

She returned home for her father's funeral in 1976. But twelve years were to elapse until the family was gathered together again as a whole – for another funeral, this time for her Uncle Harold. It was the first time John's wife, Kate, had seen Elly and Evelyn together. For Evelyn, the gathering also provided, more importantly, the beginnings of a true *rapprochement* with her mother.

Evelyn has had a similar lack of contact with her former teachers, Dorothy and Victoria Carter, though she says they are never far from her heart. In a professional sense, she regards them as more a part of her life than her family.

She is not far from their hearts, either. Victoria always remembers the first time they saw her perform with the RWB. It was in Kitchener in 1977; Evelyn was being carried onto the stage in a lift. Her foot emerged from the wings, "and I thought," says Victoria, "that's Evelyn's foot. I've corrected that foot so often, I'd know it anywhere. She just soared in on this lift, and I felt myself getting very emotional. That little girl's made it, I thought, with all the problems she's had, she's made it." Dorothy, too, talks affectionately of their former charge performing with the company in London. It was a mixed-bill evening. Evelyn was cast in every ballet except one, but that night she put on a costume for the ballet in which she didn't have a part and walked across the stage, just to be able to be in everything – "for us," says Dorothy, "for the place she had come from."

By the beginning of 1985 the partner problem was becoming a major source of friction between Evelyn and Arnold Spohr. Like many other companies, the RWB was a victim of what seemed a world-wide shortage of good, experienced, available males.

Jean Charles Gil was engaged to partner her in *Giselle* with the RWB in Winnipeg and on tour early in 1985, but Evelyn suffered another stress fracture of her ankle shortly before he arrived. Gil found himself dancing the tour opening in Vancouver with Veronica Tennant, imported as a guest, and in Edmonton and Calgary with Marianna Tcherkassky, of American Ballet Theatre. However, Evelyn joined him later on tour and in Winnipeg, and he rekindled the interest she had felt when they danced together in Marseille.

Some observers within the company found Gil mannered, but he and Evelyn got on well. He was good-looking, he had passion, he partnered her brilliantly. (Even when he once somehow tripped over the cross from Giselle's grave while carrying Evelyn, he continued to maintain the rising lifts the choreography called for. "He was falling over backward," she recalls, "with the cross coming very profanely through his legs, but he was damned if he was going to let me fall.") He seemed as keen as she was to develop a long-term performing relationship. He talked in terms of wanting to create with her something that transcended either of them as individuals. Evelyn was excited. Was this the kindred spirit she had been dreaming of?

Summer 1985 was the time when her relationship with her manager, Chuck Marahrens, began to sour. He arranged for her to do a tour of Asia, partnered by Gil, with the Universal Ballet, a Seoul-based company controlled by the Rev. Sun Yung Moon's Unification Church.

"He sold the whole kit and caboodle to the Moonies – eight dancers, the lighting designer, the stage manager, the soundman, and the company manager, which was me," says Mark Porteous. "That pushed it a little too far for Evelyn. There were other problems involving the other dancers, but of all the engagements of his that Evelyn was involved in, that was definitely the one that came closest to a big-buck opportunity."

The "other problems" that Porteous refers to had nothing to do with the Moonies (part of her contract specified that the Unification Church would not in any way attempt to "convert" her, and the only time religion ever came up was at the pre-performance prayers, in which she took no part). They included drug troubles with Patrick Bissell, who was also on the tour, though not dancing with Evelyn (an eager participant in the Moonie prayers, he was by then trying to kick the drug habit that killed him in 1987), and the crumbling of what she had hoped would be her emerging partnership with Gil.

On-stage in Korea, Japan, Taiwan, and China, dancing Roland Petit's *Proust* pas de deux and the *Giselle* second-act pas de deux, their relationship was a dream. But off-stage they were incompatible. There were noisy scenes in restaurants, and he became increasingly demanding, expecting Evelyn to look after him far beyond the requirements of a performing partnership. The more that happened, the more she retreated. "I thought, I'm not going to call you to wake you up in the morning, I'm not going to buy you a sandwich for your lunch, I'm not going to do your laundry for you, I'm your partner, not your lover," Evelyn says. "The working relationship was wonderful. But I couldn't cope with him outside."

It was shaping up to be another bleak year, the darkness only momentarily relieved in the spring of 1985 by the award of her second Nellie, the ACTRA award for best television variety performer of the year for her role in Norman Campbell's *Romeo and Juliet*. (But despite the fact that this was one of the few prizes she really wanted, she didn't attend the award event because she was "too chicken" about what she would wear.)

Throughout the 1985-86 season, the season in which she turned thirty,

Evelyn was restless, unfulfilled, consumed by indecision and self-doubt. She had become acutely aware of her age. If she was to make anything of herself internationally, it was time to get moving.

Her ambition placed her at a crossroads. She still felt loyal to the RWB, but she knew it wasn't the best place to be to advance a career as a classical ballerina. There were limits to what she could expect the company to provide in terms of the full-length classical repertoire. As well, she was eager to work with choreographers on new work – something she had only done twice in her career. After the initial excitement of Varna, she had become disillusioned with her progress. Maybe she was no longer in the right place.

By the 1985-86 season the flood of invitations to appear with other companies as a guest had dwindled to a trickle, and the few offers that did come her way fell through. An invitation to do a new ballet for Roland Petit in Marseille that December was squelched by her contractual commitment to dance in the RWB's *Nutcracker* at Christmas. A suggestion that she might join Sadler's Wells Royal Ballet on its spring tour of the U.S.A. and South America was withdrawn when the SWRB decided to save money by using guests from the Royal Ballet rather than imports.

She suffered a further emotional blow in the summer of 1986 when Chuck Marahrens died from complications arising from AIDS. His death also left her without full-time professional guidance. Since that time, Evelyn's career outside the RWB has been handled by Mark Porteous, more as a friend doing a favour than as a professional manager. Porteous is a quiet, unexcitable man with an ability to maintain grace under pressure. In conditions of conflict and stress, he prefers to find a way to make things happen rather than see them disintegrate. He's a natural diplomat. And while the strain of dealing with Evelyn would tax a less self-effacing individual, Porteous says, "When people ask why I put up with it, the answer is simple. You just sit in the audience and watch a performance. The answer is there. People ask me about benefits on the job. I can watch Evelyn Hart dance any time I want. It's a rare and incredible privilege. I have befriended one of the few true artists of my lifetime, and I will do anything that is feasible, reasonable, and necessary to protect her, assist her, and help her grow."

One of the few things that helped her grow that season, one of the bright lights in a dark year, was the company's acquisition of Jiří Kylián's pas de deux *Nuages*. His comic ballet *Symphony in D* had been a big success for the company the previous season. Now *Nuages* would become as closely identified with Evelyn as *Belong* had been.

DAVID COOPER

Evelyn and André Lewis in
Jiří Kylián's Nuages.

Jiří Kylián was born in Prague in 1947, joined the Stuttgart Ballet in 1968, and became artistic director of the Netherlands Dance Theatre in 1976. He created the original version of *Nuages*, set to the first movement of a Debussy nocturne for orchestra, for Jonas Kage and Birgit Keil for a Stuttgart Ballet gala in 1974. Like many gala pieces, it was performed once and then disappeared. In the mid-1980s it was revived in Stuttgart for another gala, this time danced by Keil and Vladimir Klos, with Reid Anderson in charge of its re-mounting. As Anderson recalls it, the revival was virtually a new version, and it brought the house down.

It was subsequently taken into the Netherlands Dance Theatre repertoire, and Evelyn and Arnold Spohr saw it in a performance in The Hague while she was making guest appearances in Amsterdam. They were both attracted to it as a pas de deux for the RWB.

Kylián's assistant, Arlette van Boven, taught it to Evelyn and André Lewis in Winnipeg, then Evelyn, Lewis, and Henny Jurriens (to facilitate the Dutch connection) travelled to The Hague to rehearse it with Kylián.

Evelyn was nervous the day of the run-through. Everyone had been warning her how intense Kylián was and how unimpressed he affected to be by the people he met, and she had interpreted these warnings as some kind of hint that he wasn't going to like *her*.

Kylián came briefly to the rehearsal room, but said he needed to be with his company and had no time to work on the piece with them. Jurriens asked him to see at least three minutes of it, but Kylián insisted he didn't have time, and got up to go. At the same moment, Arlette van Boven started the music tape, and the dancers began. Halfway to the door, Kylián stopped, turned, and looked at the dancers. Then he leaned back on the barre and watched some more. By the time they reached the thirty-second bar of the music, Kylián ordered it stopped. Evelyn's first response, thinking he didn't like it, was one of relief; she was so tense she was about to faint.

In fact, he liked it so much he sat down, began working with them immediately, and rearranged his schedule to be able to give them two hours of intense rehearsal every day for a week. "For me it was very difficult," recalls Lewis, who was called on to carry out a sustained sequence of difficult supports and manipulations as part of the duet. "The man just didn't know the word break."

Kylián's intensity intimidated Evelyn. "We went to dinner once. All of a sudden in the middle of the dinner, out of the blue, he said he had to go. People told me he had always been like that. He gets an idea and has to go and think about it."

She tried her best to come up with ideas as they worked, but never felt she was contributing anything to the piece. Kylián, however, has always credited her with taking his original idea in a completely new direction. At the end of the working period, when it came time to say goodbye, Evelyn, still convinced Kylián didn't like her, put out her hand for a handshake. Kylián laughed and gave her a big hug. "It's yours now," he said.

Despite her fears of the man, she left infatuated. "I adored him. I thought of nothing but Kylián for eight months – I fantasized about that man . . ."

Subsequently, she has come to regard Kylián as the only choreographer to understand fully where her creativity came from and to channel it to benefit the work.

Although *Nuages* is without narrative content, its nine minutes of muted modernism and softened angularities create a strong sense of rhapsodic sorrow. Lewis once said the dancers look as if they are on a cloud or the edge of a precipice, in a place of safety with danger all around; everywhere they go, they just make it before they fall. Today, it is one of very few short, abstract ballets that can touch Evelyn emotionally. Usually in the ballets she dances, she likes to manufacture a story or a relationship that she can cling to, even if there isn't one; it gives her a hook for her expressiveness. But *Nuages* is different for her every time. Sometimes she feels anger, sometimes sadness, sometimes resignation; once (in Taiwan) she found herself as she danced in a passionate mental dialogue with the choreographer.

Evelyn and Lewis gave their first performance of *Nuages* in Vancouver in

February 1986. "A showstopper," said Stephen Godfrey in *The Globe and Mail*. "Cool, abstract, emotional, and specific all at once . . . The kind of dance that becomes a signature piece." "A major addition to the RWB repertoire," said Jacob Siskind in *The Citizen* that April, "as long as someone as personally magnetic as Hart is responding to the music." And the following fall, critic William Littler wrote in *The Toronto Star*: "It is worth a trip to the O'Keefe Centre just to watch the music of Debussy flow through this body's limbs."

In the audience at the première in Vancouver was Reid Anderson, who had re-mounted the ballet in Stuttgart. "I remember thinking," he says, "this was not the *Nuages* I knew, and I knew it really well. It was something like it, but I didn't think that Evelyn really captured, at her première, a lot of -isms, Jiří-isms. But the next time I saw it, at the gala for Ballet B.C. in 1988, it had become hers, and I totally forgot anything I ever knew about *Nuages*, all I knew or wanted to know was *that Nuages*. It was totally extraordinary theatre: a few minutes in my life that I knew I would never forget. I had been associated with its predecessor, but that was something else. That gala was an evening of highlights, but people would say, *ah, but Evelyn. . . .*"

Interestingly, André Lewis is one partner with whom Evelyn had consistent success, perhaps because he was the one who came nearest to her in willing-ness and dedication. They first worked together in the school (she was in the senior year as he was beginning) and in his second year in the company he was chosen to partner her in Vicente Nebrada's *Our Waltzes*. Later they did Nebrada's *Lento a Tempo e Appassionato* together and Lewis took over as her *Belong* partner.

Part of their success together had to do with their mutual approach to music and movement. He always felt himself in tune with the way she wanted to stretch the phrases of the music and the way she wanted to be carried or placed. They spent a lot of time discussing music and interpretation, but on-stage his feeling for what she needed always took over. Their sense of together-ness was so instinctive that when he had to teach *Belong* to someone else, he had to call on Evelyn to help demonstrate it.

Partly his feeling for what she needed had to do with an understanding of the steps the woman must carry out (not all male dancers have that under-standing). Partly it was about knowing her moods – if the lights were very bright, he knew she'd be more uncomfortable; if she knew an important impresario was in the audience, that would have an influence. Partly, it was about giving and considerateness, something that was always drilled into the male students. Making the girl look good was the man's responsibility – because if the girl doesn't look good the partnering doesn't look good.

By nature calmer than Evelyn, Lewis, known in his dancing days as the company workhorse for his ability to handle as many as four ballets in a single evening, preferred to take things more easily than she did. They would rehearse before a show together, but never to excess, "because then she gets paranoid, and then I get paranoid." He always believed that his greatest strength for her was the comfort she gained from knowing that if anything went wrong, he would be able to handle it physically. Evelyn confirms that. She always trusted him.

Just before the *Nuages* première, Evelyn went with RWB dancer Barry Watt as her partner to Vancouver to dance the White Swan pas de deux at a gala in aid of the Vancouver Symphony Orchestra. Violinist Yehudi Menuhin was scheduled to accompany her, and Evelyn, acutely aware of the criticism she always received for the slowness of her tempos, was terrified that she would dance too slowly for the great musician.

At the end of the first run-through, which had actually been too fast for her comfort, Menuhin, in his gentle way, asked, "Now, dear, was that a little too slow for you?" Fighting her impulse to say it was fine simply in order to make him happy, she said, "Actually, sir, it's a little bit fast."

"Oh, *good*," said Menuhin happily. "I've seen all the best ballerinas dance it, Margot Fonteyn, Natasha – I've played it for them all. I saw Pavlova, too, and you know, no one has ever done it properly, no one has done it as slowly as Pavlova. I remember my sister telling me that Pavlova distinctly told her that it should be played very, very slowly."

So he played it the way he had been told, which was the way Evelyn had always heard it in her head, and for Evelyn it was magic. She remembers seeing Menuhin watching her dancing as he played; it felt to her as if they were melting together.

But when she enthused about the experience to RWB music director Earl Stafford, he told her she had to be crazy. He had listened to a radio broadcast of the gala and the music simply didn't work at the speed at which Menuhin played it. "If you weren't in his presence," she said, "it wasn't special. But when you were there . . . ."

The story touches on the emotional and spiritual heart of her unique musical gifts. Everyone – audiences, choreographers, critics, accompanists – talks in awed terms about Evelyn's musicality. But it is an aspect of her art that goes beyond a mere understanding of music. What we see on the stage is her emotional and spiritual response to the sounds she hears, and it is the strength and sincerity of that response that we respond to.

"It's as if she creates the music," says Rudi van Dantzig. "She doesn't dance

GLEN ERIKSON GRAPHICS

*Yehudi
Menuhin
congratulates
Evelyn after
her performance
of the White Swan
pas de deux
with Barry Watt
(left) at a
Vancouver
Symphony Orchestra
concert in 1986.
Behind Menuhin
is conductor
Kazuyoshi
Akiyama.*

to music; it comes from her. I think she absorbs the music. She inhales it first, and it exhales through her body. She also comments on the music. It's a dialogue, not merely a rhythm she moves to. It speaks a word, she speaks back. And she treats it with such care, like a mother with a child. All her senses are there when she dances."

Peter Wright says he can think of only two other dancers, Margot Fonteyn and the Royal Ballet's Merle Park, with the same depth of musical understanding as Evelyn. "You get a lot of dancers who can dance to the music, strictly on the beat," he says, "but Evelyn has a very instinctive understanding of the larger phrasing."

"Now, there are other people who are musical," says Hans van Manen, "but she uses her musicality in a very intelligent way. She has a natural feeling of time. That's a star quality; all great dancers have that. Some people dance one two three four, only one two three four. But other people can see that between the one and the two and the two and the three and the three and the four there is also so much."

"No one dances between the steps better," says Earl Stafford, who has probably been as close as anyone to Evelyn's musicality. "I've heard Evelyn criticized for being too emotional, but it never comes in the way of technique – she's got all the technique she needs to dance the way she wants to dance. It's like Rubinstein. Or Horowitz. I've heard them hit so many wrong notes, but it doesn't matter. Each of these great artists has a way of transcending that. It takes technique to a new plateau. Evelyn is in that class."

Stafford believes she was born with "a sense of music that just radiates out of her. There are some people who just cannot hear music the way Evelyn does. How many dancers are never on the music? Evelyn will never be *off* the music. If you played it, from a musician's standpoint, too fast or too slow, it wouldn't matter. She has a gift like radar vision that allows her to see what you're going to do. She becomes the musician as well as the dancer. I've never seen anyone close to it."

Questions of tempo, he says, never enter the picture. But sometimes he plays little musical games with himself. "I see her coming round the corner and I think, oh, she'll never make it. So I'll pull back a little bit and help her out . . . and I'll be late. If I had just not looked and had done my own thing, the way I should have been doing, I'd have been right on."

In fact, Stafford rarely watches the stage. He will look up at Evelyn occasionally from the pit if he wants a treat, or to get inspiration, but mostly they work in a mutually supportive independence. "To follow someone's feet," he says, "that's not where it's at. You have to do it to a certain extent – there are certain technical things you have to work with, like *fouettés* or barrel rolls, but that's not a musical role, you might as well have a tabla player or a percussionist beating time so it looks like they're on the music. They're just the tricks. The rest of the time, if you're watching, what's the music going to be doing?"

Evelyn agrees. The school of thought that suggests the pianist or conductor should follow the dancing is not one she subscribes to. "The only way you can dance," she says, "is if you follow the music. It's like a road map in front of you – you see the shapes of what you're hearing and you just follow it."

She always makes sure when she first comes to a role that she knows the music thoroughly, from listening to tapes and from score study, in order to be able to hear its shape, its pauses, and its theatricality, and relate them to the steps she has been given to do. But she doesn't for a moment consider herself an original creator. "I can't imagine," she says, "what it would be like to be a composer, to have music swirling in your head and be able to tamper with it. As a dancer, you have your own creativity, but it's within a framework. I consider myself a fixer-upper. Why don't we add that there? Isn't that so much better? Lift that up on three. Isn't that so much more theatrical?"

Even so, her remarkable ability to interpret the music she hears does not go unappreciated by the dancers in the company. "She makes me see the detail of the music," says Gino di Marco. "She makes the still moments of music look like movement." "She dances to the music that's not there to the normal ear," says Vincent Boyle, "the added notes that we don't hear."

DAVID COOPER

Evelyn with Rex Harrington in the RWB's production of Rudi van Dantzig's
Romeo and Juliet.

8 *Going to the Source*

*N*uages and Menuhin apart, by the 1985-86 season Evelyn Hart was in the doldrums.

In Winnipeg, there was little to enthral her and much to disturb her. Turned down so long before by her heart's first choice, the National Ballet School, she had transferred her loyalty to Winnipeg. All her energies had been channelled into proving how wrong Toronto's rejection was by using her talents to establish the Winnipeg company on the international map.

Yet everyone around her seemed to think that all she was out for was personal advancement. No one understood that she was deeply committed to the company, and that her insistence on becoming the best dancer she could be was her own means of carrying through that commitment.

So she turned her attention elsewhere. Back toward Toronto.

Early in 1986, she discounted publicly the suggestion that she would ever be invited to join the National Ballet. It was a matter of etiquette. The National's artistic director, Erik Bruhn, who had succeeded Alexander Grant in 1983, had been infuriated when Peter Schaufuss, as artistic director of the London Festival Ballet, had poached dancers from the National. Bruhn had made it a matter of policy never to approach a dancer who was established in another company. Even if a dancer wished to approach the National Ballet independently, Bruhn insisted that they be free of other commitments first.

But there were ways round that. Bruhn and Spohr had already negotiated a loose exchange-of-stars deal in which the RWB would get performances by Veronica Tennant and Karen Kain in return for guest appearances by Evelyn. Evelyn wanted to take it further and, with the end of her contract with the RWB approaching, offered herself to Bruhn.

Her initial idea was to work her way slowly into the company, but Bruhn advised against that. If she crossed over, he said, he would want to bring her in with a big bang in a high-profile new vehicle, and there was nothing suitable in the forthcoming season's schedule. Instead, shortly before his untimely death in April that year, he offered her a season as guest principal dancer, sharing her with the RWB.

It was the first time the two principal ballet companies had shared a ballerina, and for Evelyn the arrangement was perhaps even better than a full-scale change of companies. It relieved her of some of the pressures of being in Winnipeg (and gave the company, meanwhile, a chance to catch its breath and devote more of its attention to up-and-coming dancers); it challenged her in terms of technique and self-confidence; and it gave her easy and regular access to a broad range of classical and neo-classical works – two versions of *Romeo and Juliet*, two productions of *Giselle*, *The Sleeping Beauty*, and *Swan Lake*. It was a ballerina's dream.

Very quickly, however, the dream began to evaporate. Going from the centre of the Winnipeg spotlight to being one of the crowd in Toronto had clear disadvantages, particularly in terms of time devoted to rehearsal, coaching, and performance – precisely the problems she had encountered at Sadler's Wells in London.

The Winnipeg company, meanwhile, was concocting dreams of its own. Perhaps fearful that its one true star would slip away forever, the company revealed plans to mount a major new production of the world's most popular classical ballet in the coming season, *Swan Lake*.

And still to come was the challenge and excitement of her debut in Russia.

At an RWB performance in Red Deer, Alberta, the previous season, Martin Bazarian, the Soviet emigré musician and concertmaster of the RWB's touring orchestra, had watched the audience's thrilled response to her dancing, and told her it was time for her to be seen in Moscow.

On his own initiative, he contacted GosConcert, at that time the official organizer of appearances by visiting performers in the U.S.S.R., and persuaded the agency to authorize an invitation to Evelyn. Bazarian's ball was picked up by Toronto-based filmmaker Bob Barclay, who had made a well-received segment of the CBC-TV interview show "Gzowski & Co.", with Evelyn as the subject, filmed the previous summer and screened that January.

Barclay, working with the Canadian Embassy in Moscow, finalized the plans for Russia (an international gala showcase in Moscow and a preliminary performance in Odessa) and sold the CBC on the idea of making a film about the trip. It was a project, he argued, that would give Evelyn the kind of profile in Canada that she had deserved since Varna but had never really achieved. In a round of budget cuts, the CBC removed its backing and Barclay decided to go ahead independently, using the freelance camera crew that had filmed the television series "Peter Ustinov's Russia."

For Arnold Spohr, who accompanied Evelyn on the trip, along with Galina Yordanova as coach and partners André Lewis and John Kaminski, it was a historic moment. More than a quarter-century after his first visit to the Soviet Union in search of a style on which he could base his teaching, almost two decades after the founding of the company's Vaganova-based school, he was returning to display the crowning jewel of the school and the company: Evelyn Hart.

It marked a small but significant moment in cultural history as well: the reopening of cultural exchanges between Canada and the Soviet Union in the then-new spirit of *glasnost*, and the first time GosConcert had organized an entire evening in honour of a foreign performer.

The tour, primarily designed with Barclay's film in mind, was a hectic rush. They made a brief stop in Moscow, where Evelyn took a class at the Bolshoi Ballet with ballerina Maya Plisetskaya (whose picture had been in one of the first ballet books her mother brought her from the Peterborough public library when she was a child) and rehearsed with Andris Liepa, the rising twenty-two-year-old Bolshoi star with whom she was to dance in both Odessa and Moscow.

Then they dashed to Leningrad, home of the Kirov Ballet – but for filming, not performing. Evelyn was filmed at the Hermitage museum and took a class with the Kirov Ballet and at the Vaganova Choreographic Institute. In the main Vaganova studio, Spohr insisted that an imposing photograph of Agrippina Vaganova be taken down from its position high on the wall so that he, Evelyn, and Yordanova could be photographed beside a picture of the woman who had been, indirectly, so instrumental in building the technical quality of the RWB.

It was not the easiest of times, personally or artistically. The quality of the food was a problem, and the bureaucracy was its legendary inefficient self. In Odessa, it took fifty-four minutes (she timed it) for the trickle of lukewarm water to fill her bathtub. And at the Odessa rehearsal of *Giselle*, the corps de ballet either ignored her or laughed at her staging and interpretation.

But she found Liepa an ideal partner. Despite the fact that neither spoke each other's language, and despite the fact that they had had only one rehearsal, knew different versions of the work, brought to it different interpretations, and had never danced with the company before, Evelyn felt entirely comfortable with the Russian dancer. There wasn't anything he wouldn't try. He was open to all her ideas, and ready to offer ideas of his own, and she took that as a compliment. "He was a wonderful partner and a marvellous experience – because when you don't speak the language you have to speak through the body and through the eyes. And that's the only part of him that I remember – maybe moments in the ballet when I remember his body against mine, or his eyes, and sometimes a smile. I guess I found a fairly similar kind of artist . . . a soulmate."

Their partnership in *Giselle* on the stage of the Odessa opera house was rewarded with an ovation and twenty-five minutes of rhythmic clapping. The response in Moscow was similar, though the event itself, which also featured dancers from the Soviet Union, Bulgaria, and Australia, was chaotic. No one seemed to know what to do, so Spohr and Yordanova ended up organizing the program, choreographing the finale, staging the event, and cueing the lighting. The performing space itself, the bare, shallow stage of the Tchaikovsky Hall, a music recital hall with limited technical facilities, was not the best. Outside, the posters proclaimed Evelyn's phoneticized name in large Cyrillic lettering – ХАРТ – and zapped, she says, is how she felt.

But the sold-out house loved her. Under bright lights, curtains hanging at the back and a piano standing to the side, Evelyn opened and closed each half of the program – the White Swan pas de deux from *Swan Lake* with Liepa; *Belong* (substituted for the scheduled *Nuages* because of the splintery stage

COURTESY EVELYN HART

Evelyn,
Arnold Spohr,
and Galina Yordanova
pose with a
portrait of
Agrippina Vaganova
at the Vaganova
Choreographic
Institute,
Leningrad,
1986.

surface) with Lewis; the *Giselle* act two pas de deux with Liepa; and *Le Jazz Hot*, a lively number by RWB teacher-choreographer Jacques Lemay to Henry Mancini's music, with Kaminski.

At the end of the *Giselle* pas de deux, a tall, middle-aged man with sandy hair advanced down the aisle. He reached up to the stage and handed to Evelyn an enormous bouquet of red tulips. Evelyn bowed low to receive them.

A greater tribute could hardly have been given. The man was one of the Bolshoi Ballet's legendary former stars, Marius Liepa, father of the partner with whom she had just scored such a great success.

Evelyn returned to Canada recharged in spirit and freshly confident in her artistic reach, convinced that the trip marked a turning point in her development as an artist, a kind of coming-of-age that had given her, she said, "at least another ten years of excitement" in her career. The Odessa corps de ballet girls who had giggled when they first saw her rehearse *Giselle* had later thanked her for showing them "how it should be danced." Liepa, a star who is accustomed to being in control, had deferred to her, asking through an interpreter how she wanted to be partnered. "They were a dream of a pair, very emotional," Spohr recalled later. "He looks like a young Adonis, is tall, and Evelyn fits lovingly in his arms. It was an electric duo." Even before the trip was complete, negotiations were opened to bring Liepa to Canada to partner Evelyn in the RWB's *Giselle*.

In terms of style, she gravitated more to the Bolshoi company than the Kirov. While the Kirov is generally thought to enshrine the purest of all versions of the Vaganova technique, she found the discipline and correctness of the Kirov class and performance far less amenable than the Bolshoi version. The Kirov, she knew, is "the epitome of exquisiteness, everything is exact, all the little nuances are the same, but sometimes, while it's important to be correct with the rules, it's also important not to have the rules, to allow yourself not to be the ballerina, but to be the human being." She felt much more at home in Moscow, where everyone was allowed much more individuality; at the Kirov she felt like a radish in a tomato patch. She drew parallels between the Kirov and the Bolshoi companies and Canada's own senior troupes, likening the Kirov to the National Ballet, unified and not flamboyant, and the Bolshoi to the RWB, filled with colour and personality.

The trip's ultimate value lay in its contribution to her self-knowledge and self-confidence. In the season immediately before going to the Soviet Union she had become so nervous and unconvinced about the quality of her technique that she was seriously questioning whether she should go on

DAVID COOPER

Evelyn in Le Jazz Hot, *by Jacques Lemay.*

dancing. It felt to her like having a tooth missing at the back of her mouth; no one can see it's missing, but *she* knows.

But the coaching she had been receiving from the Moscow-trained Yordanova in Winnipeg and, more recently, the Leningrad-trained Magdalena Popa at the National Ballet, along with her performances in Odessa and Moscow, allowed her to recognize that she'd "reached the point where I finally believe I can do what other people have always said I can do. It's not dependent on anyone else. It's just dependent on me. I may fall. I may have problems technically. But I know what I have. I know I'm a ballerina."

In Winnipeg she had become acutely aware of a lack of people to turn to for advice and encouragement. And it was now that her relationship with Moroni fell into real decline.

Shortly before the Russia trip, *Belong* was filmed for use as the unifying thread in a new IMAX film on Manitoba. For Moroni and the company, the natural coupling for such a prominent piece of media display would have been the original pairing. But Evelyn insisted on dancing with André Lewis.

Similarly, news stories had announced that she would be dancing with Peregrine in Moscow. Again, their medal-winning history in normal circumstances would have made them the logical choice for such prime international exposure. For Moroni, it would have been international validation and vindication of all he had struggled for at the school. But Evelyn said no. She would never dance with Peregrine again.

At the end of 1986 Henny Jurriens became a permanent member of the Winnipeg company. Rudi van Dantzig had been grooming him for several seasons as his successor at the Dutch National Ballet, but Jurriens had become disenchanted with the density of the bureaucracy in Amsterdam, and had applied to the RWB for a position on the artistic staff. Spohr, however, persuaded the thirty-seven-year-old Jurriens to go on dancing for another couple of seasons, and he arrived that December as principal dancer and Evelyn's main partner – with their partnership in the new *Swan Lake*, in May 1987, as the season's crowning glory.

In charge of the new *Swan Lake*, logistically the most challenging production ever mounted by the RWB, was Galina Yordanova. Spohr asked her to make a *Swan Lake* that would strip away the many modifications made this century and return to the spirit of the production created by Petipa and Ivanov in St. Petersburg in the mid-1890s.

In Yordanova, Evelyn found not only a teacher and choreographer but a supporter and a guide. They shared tenacity and drive for perfection and, more than that, Yordanova had an understanding of Evelyn's insecurities. Evelyn compared their relationship to Annie Sullivan and Helen Keller – the teacher and the blind pupil, one-to-one, twenty-four hours a day.

The new *Swan Lake* was not only another career highpoint, it was a source of deep expressive satisfaction. Evelyn sees the narrative classics as the true foundation of ballet, and while she agrees that the stories are preposterous, she argues that (as in classical theatre) it is up to the performers to make them relevant to their society and age. Audiences don't go to the ballet to see a story, she says. "They go to be involved in the basics of human life – love, relationships, sorrow, happiness, hope, struggle, nobility, dignity, innocence – and I really believe that people today are searching for that. Classical ballet is a very powerful and spirit-healing thing."

Interestingly, she sees the real star of *Swan Lake* as the corps de ballet, not the ballerina in the lead – because "there is something about a group of people who struggle mentally and physically to create a unified thing that is unbelievably inspiring and touching and powerful to any human being who watches it."

Her relationship with the National Ballet of Canada remained a troubled one, complicated by the fact that a foot injury in the fall of 1987 meant she had to cancel several weeks of work, including her role as the Swan Queen in the National Ballet's *Swan Lake*. She maintained her connections with the company, sharing the lead in *The Merry Widow* with Karen Kain when the company performed in Winnipeg at the start of the season, and returning in May 1988, dancing her first Tatiana in John Cranko's *Onegin*, opposite Rex Harrington.

One of the reasons Evelyn had wanted to go as a guest to the National Ballet was the hope that she would be able to travel with the company to performances in the world's dance capitals and thus get the kind of international exposure that the Winnipeg company didn't provide. In fact, the Toronto company has never taken her on tour outside the country, and from the company's point of view it would have made no sense to do so. It had a host of established and rising ballerinas of its own to keep satisfied.

But Evelyn believes the company never genuinely wanted her as a guest. She felt she was invited simply out of obligation, because of the status she had gained in Canada. She also believes the company's coolness toward her is connected to her initial rejection by the National Ballet School, and to what she has rationalized as one of the reasons for that rejection – that her manner of working "just doesn't fit into their scheme of things."

There was also the element of competition. As a guest in a large company, she always felt she had to prove herself afresh each time she danced, because each time she danced she was taking away someone else's performance. Even so, she bristled against suggestions that her interpretations were wrong (when she danced Balanchine's abstract *Serenade* with the company, she says, she was reprimanded by a member of the artistic staff for giving it too much emotion).

What she most resented was that the company's manner of working didn't allow her time to be properly prepared for the challenges of the roles she danced. She needed rehearsal time to be able to come to a performance calm.

To some performers, professionalism lies in pulling off a show with the least amount of effort. Evelyn considers that irresponsible to both art and audience, partly because of the simple physical challenge of it all. She believes the artist must strive for more light and shade, more expressiveness, as long as improvement is possible. The transition from the rehearsal room to the stage in classical ballet is a difficult one. Suddenly, the ballerina is standing on one toe and spinning round in a costume that completely restricts her movement and is quite unlike practice garb. Often, a ballerina wearing a tutu will have no clear idea of where the floor is; when she leaps about the stage she's leaping blind. (For that reason, Evelyn prefers not to use the rehearsal-room mirror when she prepares a role; that way, she doesn't get used to using the mirror for balance.)

On-stage it's always different from rehearsal, she believes, but it's never better, because it's in the rehearsal hall that the dancer first has the vision of what can be done. Ideally, by the time it reaches the stage, that initial vision has been repeated a thousand times and has become an ingrained response. To achieve an impact that puts people's hearts in their mouths, the dancer's mind must be relaxed and in complete control – not merely able to do the step, but able to feel in calm command of its technicalities. She draws parallels between herself and Fred Astaire: Astaire would put weeks of solid work into a five-minute number, using hard effort to gain an effect of natural artistry.

Her enforced inability to have the comfort and the cushion of that preparation lay at the heart of her discontent in Toronto. When she did her first performance of Balanchine's *Concerto Barocco* she had an anxiety crisis. Balanchine has never been her favourite choreographer, and she had had none of the rehearsal time that is necessary to build a ballet of this kind into the body's muscle-memory. (She still doesn't believe the National Ballet dances Balanchine's work very well, because it isn't rehearsed enough.)

Having to do the first run-through of a ballet in front of an audience was like having to put your kitchen-work on the stage. "You need to have a place where you can scratch and pick your nose. Kids don't get toilet-trained in public. They do it in private until finally they're ready to step out. And it *is* that personal, at least to me it is."

She only had one full dress rehearsal in all her time at the National, for her debut in *Onegin*, "and the only reason I got it was that they knew if they didn't promise me a dress rehearsal I wouldn't show up in Toronto."

She believes she made herself unpopular by making the dancers around her realize that they were not being treated as well as they might be. The year she was there as guest principal, she noticed that "everybody started complaining about not having rehearsals and getting a lot more temperamental. I think I just upset the whole business."

Her intensity and drive for perfection also earned her a reputation as a

DAVID STREET

Evelyn as Tatiana with Rex Harrington as Onegin in the National Ballet of Canada's production of John Cranko's ballet.

"difficult" partner within the company. Other than Rex Harrington, she believed, no one was keen to dance with her. But she rapidly discovered that dancing with Harrington made all the other drawbacks fade into insignificance.

If it seems that love and partnering are inextricably entangled for Evelyn Hart, nowhere is that more clearly seen than in her dancing relationship with Harrington. They first danced together when she guested in the 1986-87 season, performing Balanchine's *Four Temperaments* and some abstract works. Then, in the spring of 1988, they were cast in John Cranko's romantic tragedy, *Onegin*, and the sparks began to fly. Deirdre Kelly in *The Globe and Mail* called the partership "a heavenly match," and William Littler in *The Toronto Star* said: "With Hart one didn't seem to be watching a dancer performing steps . . . What one saw was the character, the woman caught up by an image of romance, who surrenders to it, is rebuffed by it and in time tearfully turns her own back on it." Watching them together, Henny Jurriens compared them to the early years of the Fonteyn-Nureyev partnership, and late that year invited Harrington to Winnipeg to dance *Swan Lake* with Evelyn.

Suddenly, for Evelyn, everything seemed to be falling into place. He was the "pure dance spirit" she had been searching for. She trusted him instantly; he seemed to have an instinctive understanding of what she wanted. She didn't have to explain quality of movement, musicality, balance, position: he was a natural. She was also attracted by his emotional honesty on the stage. He was one of the few people she could look directly in the eye. No wall.

He was quick, too, to understand her commitment to her roles and her need to believe in them for the duration of her time on the stage. In one of their last performances of *Onegin* in Toronto in the fall of 1988, at a point in the ballet where Onegin, the seducer, is supposed to whisper in the ear of the heroine, Tatiana, Harrington whispered to Evelyn, "I love you." He never did it again, but she saw it as his recognition of her need to speak during a performance, to reinforce emotion with action.

She appreciated the quickness of his physical response to music, and its similarity to hers. His imagination saw the shapes of the music in the same way. And he had an instinctive response to her body. Suddenly she could do things that she had never been able to do before. That frightened her, not because she thought that it might disappear, but because of what it implied for the future of their partnership. Working with him made her realize there was a dimension of the art that she still hadn't been able to touch.

What was it like to dance with him? "I'm totally secure, and yet I'm on eggs. Someone said to me, it sounds like love. You stand in the wings, feeling really nervous, but you know you really want to do the performance. Sounds like love. And you get out there and after a few minutes you realize that everything's all right and you're having a good time. Sounds like love. With Rex I have this instinctive sense that I have to put myself on the line like never before. What takes it into the added dimension is the sense of risk. Everybody said, 'Weren't you frightened up there – he just throws you around.' I said, 'He was?' I feel velocity, but I don't feel the fear of velocity. And then I realize what I'm doing with him up there, and I realize that the more I relax the better it will be. It is knowing you are going to be forced to go a step further than you know is comfortable, with the person you know you want to take that step with. Perhaps it *is* the same as being in love. There's something that happens inside me when I'm with Rex that makes me feel like a complete woman on the stage. I feel vulnerable, I feel strong, I feel totally free to be 100 per cent me. It's also a physical thing . . . the way he holds me, the way he touches me, what he conveys through the way he touches me."

In *Swan Lake*, for instance, she had always wanted to add "a physical dimension of love." She believed she had found, within the ballet vocabulary that is used in the Black Swan pas de deux, a sexual awakening for the character – a real sexuality that adds another dimension to the Swan Queen's vulnerability. Harrington was the only partner so far with whom she had ever been able to bring out this aspect of the role.

For his part, Harrington felt he had finally found someone who breathed and danced and felt the way he did. "We're so in touch with each other that it's amazing," he told me in the spring of 1989, "and it's getting really difficult to dance with anyone else." He talked about the partnership in terms of an emotional relationship, not just an on-stage one. The intensity of the encounter, he said, was like two souls meeting.

Like Evelyn, he is acutely aware of the barrier of imaginary glass that so often comes between two dancers and prevents them from reaching out fully to each other on the stage. Harrington has danced with most of the National Ballet ballerinas of recent times, but in many cases (not all) "I could look into people's eyes and they'd look away because they don't want that connection. Evelyn just eats that up, and I eat that up with her . . . it's an emotional level that some people just can't reach, I guess. I've danced with people who never even look at you throughout the whole pas de deux, or they're gazing right through you, and I think that radiates to the audience. But with Evelyn there are no barriers. My heart goes. It's a feeling that when we get together it becomes our own world. You almost forget there's an audience." (The only other person he ever felt a comparable connection with was Veronica Tennant, "in that when I looked into her eyes there was a connection that came from within . . . like spirits, meeting.")

"I think a lot of men have trouble with that aspect of it," he said. "They're much more into doing the twenty pirouettes and the tricks. But for me, baring the soul is something I'm really comfortable with on the stage. Why sit and watch someone do a circus act? I'd rather reach someone emotionally and have them remember a feeling. I never cry, watching dance. I hate watching dance, because I dance, and I get so frustrated. But I watch her do [Hans van Manen's] *Adagio Hammerklavier* and I cry. I see her do *Nuages*, it puts me in tears."

The magic of their relationship was not lost on their audience.

"If I missed seeing you two dance together I would be sorely tempted to slit my wrists," wrote one fan after a performance they did in Toronto. "Individually you are both outstanding dancers. Together you create something so beautiful it is almost painful . . .

"I know Winnipeg would probably drop a bomb on Toronto if you ever moved to Toronto permanently, Miss Hart, and I, for one, would weep buckets should you, Mr. Harrington, ever move to Winnipeg, but my greatest joy would be to see you dance together on a more regular basis. It is utterly amazing to think, here you are from different schools, different ages, substantially different heights, dancing with different companies . . . yet this partnership is a wondrous, precious thing."

In the summer of 1988, Evelyn was invited to be part of the World Ballet Festival in Japan, an international extravaganza featuring the cream of the

DAVID COOPER

Evelyn with Henny Jurriens in Hans van Manen's Adagio Hammerklavier.

world's crop: seventeen couples, in ten performances that included two productions of *Swan Lake* with different principals for each of the four acts. Evelyn danced act two with Henny Jurriens, and also danced during the festival with Stephen Hyde, a principal dancer from the RWB. "They always say these things are like a school recital," she says. "Ha. Ha. Ha. It's kamikaze. Even getting a rehearsal is hard."

Hyde found the preparations for the galas in Japan gruelling. At first he was nervous, because of who Evelyn was, and he was scared to do anything with her, in case he made a mistake and made her unhappy. At Evelyn's level of dedication, it seemed that nothing could be done right; there wasn't much room for human error. There were times when he was ready to quit. But the reward lay in the finished performance. Dancing with her brought more out of him as a partner and as an expressive stage presence. It would always bring him back for more, and the more he returned, the more he blossomed as an artist.

For Evelyn, performing again in Japan was like a homecoming. Her affection for the Japanese audience dates back to the Osaka contest in 1980 and her subsequent guest appearances with the Homura Tomoi company and the Universal Ballet. "They're the first public that hasn't been afraid to stand up and say, We think you're world class and we appreciate what you do. We don't care what the London or New York public says, this is what we believe and what we receive."

Her adulation in Japan takes many forms. Audience members write effusive letters praising her performances, they send her photographs of themselves, they shower her with flowers and gifts. During the RWB's tour of the Orient early in 1988, she was asked to plant a tree to mark the start of the plum blossom festival in Setagaya, a ward of Tokyo that is twinned with Winnipeg.

Unhappy that Setagaya didn't have a theatre at which the company could perform, the community compensated with the full royal treatment "for the Swan." The Canadian flag was flying as she arrived at city hall to be greeted by the mayor, two deputy mayors, and the ward chairman. As our small party (Evelyn, Mark Porteous, Winnipeg radio journalist Jacqui Good, and myself) walked through the corridors, the staff stood at their office doorways, applauding. In the mayor's parlour, an abundance of Winnipeg memorabilia was prominently displayed; Evelyn promised to send a pair of her toe-shoes to add to the collection. At the park, a hundred Japanese schoolchildren, waving Canadian flags and singing "It's a Small, Small World" in Japanese, formed an honour guard of welcome and draped each of us with double garlands of origami cranes and bouquets of roses. The tree-planting was followed by a tea ceremony in Evelyn's honour.

"I've never felt more like Princess Di in my life," she said. "Imagine being royalty – when just the fact that you're alive is enough for people to get excited about."

Beyond the special connection she has with the Japanese audience, she also feels a bonding with the country and the people. She gravitates instinctively to the Japanese preoccupation with matters of the spirit and the intellect. The Japanese passion for simplicity, beauty, and perfection gives her new insights into her own art, she says, and into her own spiritual interior. To catch a moment in nature, as Japanese artists can, is to wipe away everything negative and put her in touch with "something eternal."

Evelyn's performances at the *Swan Lake* extravaganza in Tokyo particularly impressed another of the participants, Peter Schaufuss, then principal dancer and artistic director of the London Festival Ballet, and he invited her to partner him in a new LFB film version of *Swan Lake*, choreographed by Natalia Makarova and about to be made in Denmark.

"In Tokyo," Schaufuss told the media when the announcement was made, "I realized that she is one of the best ballerinas today and especially unique as Odette/Odile." But Evelyn had not been his first choice for the role, and when she turned up to begin rehearsals in Aarhus that August, she and Makarova immediately began to have severe differences over how the role should be interpreted.

It was not a happy time. Despite her diffidence in Makarova's presence, Evelyn consistently stood up for her own view of the work (and was heartened on occasion to see Makarova on the side trying out things she had suggested). But she felt under constant psychological pressure. Schaufuss rarely rehearsed with her, sending in dancer Paul Chalmers as his deputy for preparation shots and only coming onto the set when it was time to film. When Evelyn wasn't able to hit all thirty-two of the *fouettés* in her variations, Makarova insisted that she try them again and again. When Evelyn protested that she needed to rest, Makarova simply scoffed, "But you are young." At one

Children present Evelyn with flowers and origami leis at a tree-planting ceremony in Tokyo, 1988.

MAX WYMAN

point, Evelyn burst into tears and ran behind the scenery to cover her dismay. Out on the studio floor, she heard Makarova exclaim, "Now she is hiding from me." Midway through the two-week filming schedule, Evelyn considered a sleeping-pill overdose as a way to get herself out.

At the same time, Makarova demonstrated a high professional regard for the nervous young Canadian. Henny Jurriens, who was accompanying Evelyn, recalled the way the Russian reacted when she first saw Evelyn dance. It was like the time when Jiří Kylián first stopped by the barre in the studio in The Hague to watch her do *Nuages*, he said. Watching a tape playback one day, Makarova turned to Evelyn and told her: "Two, three years, you will be the top." Early in 1990, Makarova sent her a warm note of congratulation and encouragement. And as difficult as she found rehearsals with a stand-in, Evelyn came away from the experience with a deep respect for Peter Schaufuss. Ultimately, she had been able to reach with him that all-important performance connection, when the invisible barrier came down and the performance went beyond a partnership and became the portrayal of a relationship.

In retrospect, Evelyn can joke about the experience. She does a wicked Makarova imitation as she tells her stories, fist on pushed-out hip, imaginary cigarette adangle from the corner of her mouth, puffing the smoke upward. But at the time it was distressing and humiliating.

Acutely aware of her position at the head of her company, feeling a responsibility to set standards against which her colleagues could measure themselves, and deeply disappointed with her actual performance on the film, Evelyn returned to Winnipeg in anguish. She felt she had let everyone down. Her self-esteem was so low she imagined fellow dancers were pointing fingers and whispering that she couldn't dance a step. What made matters worse was that she had to go out, in *Concerto Barocco* and her first performances that October of *The Dying Swan*, and prove herself all over again. Just as things picked up, they always seemed to be shot down again.

9 Exits and Entrances

velyn learned *The Dying Swan* at Henny Jurriens's request. Originally choreographed by Michel Fokine for Anna Pavlova for a gala in St. Petersburg in 1907, it is danced to the solo cello variation for the swan from Saint-Saens's *Carnival of the Animals*. It is brief and evocative, barely begun before it is over, yet to many dance lovers the world over it is the epitome of ballet's grace, beauty, and emotional appeal.

Despite its brevity, it proved to be one of the most difficult achievements of Evelyn's career, not in terms of technique (it is comparatively undemanding) but in terms of interpretation.

She learned it first from Yordanova, but after seeing the scratchy and incomplete film of Pavlova dancing the role, made a number of changes designed to give her own rendering some of the spirit of innocence and beauty that she saw in Pavlova's performance. Her changes were not welcomed by the RWB's artistic staff. Yordanova kept urging Evelyn to abandon the "primitive" Pavlova version and go back to the more recent and more sophisticated version by Maya Plisetskaya, complete with added arabesques and other frills. Evelyn balked at the idea. Pavlova's version had, along with the beauty, the emotional bluntness that she was seeking. In the end, she did it her own way.

From time to time critics and other observers have found Evelyn's dancing mannered. Richard Cragun says he was at one time worried that her best

Evelyn in The Dying Swan.

DAVID COOPER

attributes – her expressiveness, her emotional strengths – were becoming overdone. Betty Oliphant goes into raptures about her musicality and her lyricism, but finds her acting (in the first act of *Giselle*, for instance) excessive. David Y. H. Lui thinks she sometimes draws out musical tempi to the point where the music suffers.

But serious parallels might be drawn again here between Evelyn and Pavlova, the dancer she admires and emulates most of all. A critic in *The Times* of London, reviewing Pavlova's *Giselle*, talked about the "wild intensity about her miming in the scene of her madness and death which is at once heart-rending and subduing."

Evelyn admits she has had a tendency to overdo things, particularly when she is just starting in a role or is in her first rehearsal in a ballet she hasn't done for a while. But it is all too easy for the onlooker to confuse sincerity with artifice, particularly in a performer of such extreme sincerity as Evelyn Hart. What she aims for on the stage is a kind of natural guilelessness, the opposite of artifice. And those who complain about her Odette or her Giselle are really complaining about Evelyn herself. She doesn't consciously try to change her expressions or her emotions, she merely puts her full self, body and emotions, into the role.

She recognizes the drawbacks in that approach and works persistently to pare down what she brings to the performance, but nervousness can inhibit her natural instinct, and so can her chronic lack of self-confidence. To have the strength to take to the stage in the personage of one of ballet's grand tragic figures presupposes a certain strength of self-belief. The more she can believe in herself, the freer she will be to create less and less that is artificial.

She is convinced, however, that what comes from inside is as important as superimposed technique. "People who want flash and dash; that's fine, those people are around, but that's really not the art of ballet, that's more gymnastics. The fact that the people who excel in the ballet world are often the ones who excel technically can sometimes be a confusing message to young dancers and to the public.

"But if you find a performance that combines amazing artistry with technique that is not necessarily brilliant but not distracting, then the public really recognizes it. It's not so easily stampable as sensational. The feelings these performances evoke are much more human and mortal, so that people, even if they're touched by it, aren't so impressed by it as if they saw people turning on their heads a hundred times. But they will remember it when they go home."

Equally, she believes, the creation of character comes from within the individual, not without. Coloration of a role might be dictated to a certain extent by experience, but the essence is inbred in the artist. It isn't necessary to have lived through an experience to be able to portray it; you don't have to commit murder to be able to imagine the act. That's why she considers it so important to stay in touch with the innocent child within herself. Even the heartache she sometimes feels is part of the creation of beauty.

"There *is* a greater being, and you become aware of that when you see great dance or hear great music. You feel your soul, to the point where you think it's going to burst. At those moments time stands still and it's not possible to feel more. You are conscious of your whole spiritual and physical being. It's the same as making love – it's all-consuming."

It is perhaps a mark of Evelyn's generosity and openness of spirit that two of the women she most admires as artists and as friends are the two women who might most logically have been considered her greatest rivals in Canadian dance, Veronica Tennant and Karen Kain, of the National Ballet of Canada.

Her relationship with Veronica Tennant, the dancer whose television Juliet first inspired Evelyn to think of dancing, has been one of mutual warmth, support, and admiration since their first encounter at a gala in Ottawa in 1981.

When Evelyn danced her first Giselle with the National Ballet of Canada, Veronica was there to wish her luck. The two women have always had an instinctive understanding. There are no mysteries between them, and no sense of rivalry. They have always shared (and admired in each other) the sense of having had to fight for what they have achieved. And they admire similar things about each other, above all the sincerity that is communicated on the stage, a sincerity that transcends the technicalities.

They care for each other's careers, and exchange gifts for good luck. Once Veronica gave Evelyn some pearls because Evelyn had always admired her pearl earrings. When Veronica danced Aurora in *The Sleeping Beauty*, Evelyn gave her a thimble (the ideal present, you might think, for a girl fated to sleep for a hundred years because of a thumb-prick) and a greeting card with a wheel on the cover turned to the appropriate age. Evelyn had turned it to sixteen: happy sixteenth birthday for the sleeping beauty.

They are drawn to each other by their likenesses and their differences. Both bring a commitment to their artform that goes far beyond personal gratification. They consider themselves servants of the dance. They have often commiserated over their frustrations: their penchants for working harder than most of the people around them, their fears that if they don't handle a situation well their partners will rebel, their disappointments over dogmatic coaching.

Yet right to the end of Tennant's performing career they presented very

JIM HAMMEL

Evelyn with Rex Harrington in the RWB's *production of* Swan Lake.

different personas on the stage. Evelyn's art is all extrovert emotional expressiveness; Veronica's was cooler, more restrained. Unlike Evelyn, Veronica never just let her instincts flow. What she accomplished on the stage, despite these restrictions, was a product of instinct and courage.

The two women also had differences of approach that both were quick to recognize and benefit from. Veronica was able to learn from Evelyn's habit of assuming an entire character as if it were her own. When Veronica was having trouble with the title role in *The Merry Widow* Evelyn gave her new insight into how she could correlate her understanding of herself with her vision of the widow. Contact with what she calls Evelyn's "seething intelligence," and the chance to see the task of dancing through Evelyn's eyes, enlarged her view.

Ultimately, although each recognized the great talent in the other, and the agonies that came with it, both knew the limitations of the help they could bring. Evelyn learned to stay away from the dressing room immediately before Veronica was due to go on stage, as it was the time when her friend was at her most nervous, and most in need of being alone. And when Evelyn was dancing *Swan Lake* with the National Ballet, suffering agonies of nerves and insecurity, Veronica knew she could comfort her only to a point. Beyond that, the troubles were Evelyn's alone to bear.

Karen Kain has been another inspirational support. When Evelyn guests in Toronto, she likes to share a dressing room with Karen. She finds it reassuring.

In many ways, Evelyn's career has followed – a few years behind – in Kain's footsteps. Karen, too, knows what it's like to carry the weight of the box office, to be rushed around the world doing guest work, to have to carry the responsibilities that come with international medal-winning acclaim. When Evelyn returned, her self-esteem in tatters, from taping the Makarova *Swan Lake* in Denmark in 1988, one of the first people she met was Karen. Still in shock, Evelyn poured out her troubles. Karen was immediately understanding, sympathetic, consoling. Evelyn felt she had a big sister, someone who understood, someone who had gone through similar experiences. It made her feel better about what she had considered a failure.

From her earliest years as a dance student, one of Evelyn Hart's dreams was to become a performer who would "put Canada on the map." When the people at the National Ballet school in effect told her they wanted no part of her future, she switched her loyalties and her energies to Winnipeg, and her desire to succeed internationally on behalf of Canada became stronger than ever – in part, to prove to the people in Toronto that they had been wrong about their decision.

Her success at Varna was that proof, and throughout the 1980s she was the Royal Winnipeg Ballet's undisputed star. Her effect on the company was undeniable; perhaps she was its salvation. Without Evelyn, the company would never have been inspired (or able) to add the major classical works to its repertoire. Opinions remain mixed on the importation of the classics for the RWB; costs of mounting a big production are so high the company is always being forced to cut costs and trim production values on tour with the classics, so Winnipeg is the only place that gets the full treatment. But general manager Bill Riske, tracking the sales through the 1980s, was under no delusions about the way Evelyn enhanced the RWB's saleability, particularly when the company was touring a full-length ballet.

Inevitably, Evelyn found herself cast as a role-model within the company, despite the fact that she felt constantly threatened by most of her colleagues. At the same time, she recognized and welcomed the responsibilities that stardom imposed on her within the company, and she was generous to dancers she felt were not merely trying to compete with her but were working to develop themselves as individual artists.

Evelyn's ambitions for her colleagues are rooted in her belief in the need for total dedication to the artform. She wants to "strengthen and encourage other people's love-affairs toward their own art. To help them have the courage to get past their worries about whether they're good enough, and just dance for their art's sake. I have no time for dancers who have disrespect for their artform. I know I have no right to say anything to them, so I keep it inside, but I want to say, get out of this profession – you are a detriment to this profession, you don't belong here."

The trappings of stardom are things she expects as her right – a dressing room of her own, the freedom to come and go in the studio at any hour, and the staff support to help her develop her technique at an international level. At the same time, she likes to be looked on as "a fellow soldier, a part of the unit." Despite her successes, her acclaim, the mounting evidence of her uniqueness, she has always been totally un-starlike in her relations with other dancers, either in Winnipeg or in companies where she has appeared as a guest. Often, she will go off into a corner with someone and work privately on an aspect of their technique or interpretation. If a dancer is doing a new role for the first time, you will often find Evelyn in the wings, capering about and pulling funny faces to help relieve the first-performance tension.

Her success has not always been easy for the dancers. Initially, the urge to be thin in emulation of Evelyn was epidemic. Anorexia became increasingly a problem at the school as Evelyn became increasingly important, and it overlapped into the company as students graduated. Slowly, however, the trend died down as dancers realized that physical appearance was not what they should be aiming to emulate.

But everyone at every level in the company has felt the effect of her presence. A dancer might be scheduled for rehearsals for a demi-soloist role and find herself bumped from the studio because Evelyn decides she wants to change her own rehearsal times. If this happens more than once or twice, the dancer is going to get to opening night under-rehearsed. It wouldn't be a problem in a company with the space and resources to absorb that kind of logistical upset, but at the tiny RWB the potential damage is magnified. "I don't think it's going to kill anyone," says Lendre Rodgers Kearns, "I don't think it's ruined anyone's career, but there has been a lot of sacrifice for Evelyn's career that Evelyn will never know about."

In fact, given the things Evelyn has done and the way she has radically modified the RWB's look and repertoire, there is little jealousy or resentment of her within the company (though the twenty-six-member RWB is not a company in which grudges can be carried for long – with everyone thrown together in constant close proximity, disagreements must flare up and die in a matter of days). Rather, the Winnipeggers take a quiet pride in what she has achieved. Company member Gino Di Marco talks of watching her performances as "like a still moment in your life." Vincent Boyle says: "I can't say how many thousands of times I've watched her, yet I've never seen a show and said, 'This wasn't very good tonight.' You just don't watch Evelyn and say that."

By 1989 Evelyn knew full well that she was going to have to leave Winnipeg if she seriously wished to achieve her own goals as an artist. Ideally, perhaps, she should have been given the freedom to fulfil herself by developing a performing relationship with a prominent artist outside the company, a dancer such as Richard Cragun, who is more mature in years and performance, and who could carry her upward as an artist – and at the same time help to make her famous. (Ironically, Cragun once asked if he could have her as his partner for a *Romeo and Juliet* performance in Zurich, and was told by the Zurich management that they loved her very much but she didn't have enough of an audience.)

It would be easy to cast the people at the RWB as self-interested manipulators holding her back from these opportunities. But for many of those years she lacked the self-confidence to grasp them and clung, instead, to her Winnipeg security-blanket. The RWB is a small company in a small city; her star position allowed her an undemanding comfort. Winnipeg also let her work without pressure. She didn't have to run around all over the place to find good classes, the way she might have had to in New York, and she didn't have to fight to prove herself in the face of constant competition. In those early years, she needed someone to look after her. Whenever she went somewhere alone, it was devastating for her.

Arnold Spohr draws a parallel between Evelyn and a former dancer with the Dutch National Ballet, a ballerina who shared Evelyn's quality and fragility. She became anorexic, then turned to liquor, "and died a year or two later because there was no one to look after her." Evelyn could easily have left the RWB, Spohr agrees, but "anywhere else she would probably have been crushed. We gave her love, lots of love, and she blossomed. But no one gets anything for nothing. God gives us crosses to bear. She has her fears, her demons, but she fights them down."

Evelyn herself was acutely aware of her fears and demons. Challenge demolished her. When the Kirov company crossed Canada and people talked about how sensational the Kirov ballerinas were, she automatically felt inferior. She feels, too, the loneliness of striving to be better as an artist and never knowing for sure if the improvements are happening. For a soul as sensitive as Evelyn's, one bad rehearsal is worth twenty good ones; one negative comment wipes out a hundred positive ones.

Experience, too, had been a painful teacher. She was convinced that her

1984 guest engagement in London with Sadler's Wells Royal Ballet (an engagement she had hoped would raise her international profile) was a disaster. Nothing had ever seemed to go right at the National Ballet of Canada. The Makarova *Swan Lake* taping was an enduring embarrassment – to her, if not to anyone else.

The structure of the Canadian ballet network, with the National Ballet of Canada securely established as the main event and the RWB and Les Grands Ballets Canadiens in Montreal relegated to subsidiary roles, almost certainly contributed to Evelyn's relative lack of international acclaim. Karen Kain became a big star because she was with the National Ballet, dancing in the country's principal city and performing the kind of roles people expect a classical prima ballerina to dance. Evelyn was dancing such pieces as *Mahler Four: Eternity Is Now* and *Five Tangos* in a small city on the edge of the prairies, or on tour in small towns.

She was also held back by the lack of anyone to guide her in the basic details of what to do, who to go to, and how to go about it. After Chuck Marahrens's death, she lacked the assistance of a full-time manager able to deal with her as an individual and at the same time open the doors wide enough to enable her (or pressure her) to move toward greater international recognition.

On a purely personal level, the Winnipeg company also provided the sense of family that her own family couldn't. It was the one place in the world where she had a history, where she felt safe to fail. She has sometimes defended her decision to stay there for so long with artistic arguments rooted in her loyalty to the company and her belief, developed over the years of dancing its repertoire, that "oftentimes our quality is more to the heart of the work than the best of the major centres of the world." In Winnipeg, unlike New York, there was no pressure on the company to conform to the stylistic fad of the month. "It is important to me to maintain the standards of ballet artistry: people pay so much to see so little. If I were to go to New York I might have money or be more famous, but whether or not I would be able to be a true artist is the question." There was also, simply, her loyalty to Canada. She wanted to succeed for her country.

Not everyone believed she should leave Winnipeg. "Where should she have gone?" asks Hans van Manen. "In the dance world everybody knows her and regards her as a fantastic dancer. How many stars are there today? Look at all those galas, all those fantastic pas de deux that years ago only a few people could do. How many people can you name of that quality of her generation? Royal Ballet? None. In France, Sylvie [Guillem, of the Paris Opéra Ballet, who later moved to the Royal Ballet in London]. In Germany, only in Stuttgart. So it is perfect. You don't go to New York any more. You don't need to."

Richard Cragun, who became an international star while anchoring his career to a company in a small town in Germany, thought it "wise and healthy for her to stay where she grows. She isn't one of those warhorses who should go round the world battling through the commercial department," cashing in on her celebrity by turning out one guest-star *Don Quixote* or *Belong* after another. Marcia Haydée, Cragun's partner for many years, Evelyn's early idol, and now artistic director at Stuttgart, is a perfect example of how success doesn't depend on location. She, too, spent her career in Stuttgart, and she believes she could never have had the same career in New York or London "because the stress is too big. And the stress has nothing to do with competition, it has to do with the everyday life in those places – it's a fight in itself, and it doesn't allow enough time or peace for development. Some of us are lucky enough to have found a place that is blessed with a still, lighter atmosphere that allows us to develop. That's what happened for me here and that's what happened for Evelyn in Winnipeg."

Rudi van Dantzig believes that staying in Winnipeg gave Evelyn a stable hiding-place where she could develop her career at her own pace. He agrees she should be better known internationally, but he makes the point that the dance boom of the 1980s put a glut of dancers on the market, making the potential for any one individual's international stardom less likely. "The times of Nureyev and Fonteyn seem to be gone," he says. "Once, every man in the street knew Nureyev's name; but today many people don't know who Baryshnikov is. Had Evelyn with her qualities lived fifteen years earlier, her name would have been very different."

From the end of 1986 on, when Henny Jurriens joined the company as a principal dancer, she also had a creative reason to stay in Winnipeg. For what she considered the first time, she had a partner she could grow with. He held the promise of the future; and it could be realized on her home soil.

When Jurriens succeeded Arnold Spohr as artistic director of the company in the summer of 1988, Evelyn soon overcame her disappointment at the loss of him as partner, because she now found an important new collaborator in her creative endeavours. The extensive period they had spent dancing together enabled him to take a realistic view of her demands in the rehearsal studio. He recognized that, for Evelyn, every rehearsal is like a performance, and as artistic director he was more easily able to mollify disgruntled partners who might have been upset by what seemed like her intransigence. To have someone in the workplace who understood her that well was a wonderful gift. And their background together allowed him to give her direction without detracting from her own sense of creativity or making her feel threatened as a performer.

Late in 1988, her Uncle Harold, wife of Maxine's sister Mary, died. Evelyn, always reluctant to let anything get in the way of her work, debated at first whether she should go to the funeral. But both Porteous and Henny Jurriens felt it was important for her to attend. "If you're really interested in getting rid of something from the past," Jurriens told her, "you have to go." Porteous finally insisted, and literally drove her to the plane.

Her return to Mitchell for her uncle's funeral proved to be an important marker, a watershed in her relationships with her family. She hadn't been near the town for eight years. Nevertheless, by the very fact of her being there, she was letting her Aunt Mary know how much the loss meant to her. Beyond that, though, she felt she was returning to her family. With them, she discovered afresh their essential Christian goodness and, within herself, a new compassion and love for them. For the first time since she was a child, she felt a part of her family, sharing their vision of the way things are and might be – a vision that has to do with what she terms "an unconditional love for humanity" and a reverence for the human spirit, "humility, compassion, sensitivity, humour, joy, belief in beauty and innocence" – a vision of sharing that provides the entire *raison d'être* of her expressiveness on the stage.

She knew that they loved her and had supported her since the beginning. The negative forces that had kept her away from her family, from her mother in particular, were, she finally realized, as much her own making as anyone else's.

She returned to Winnipeg with a lighter step. A load had been abandoned. She was at peace with her roots at last.

There is a photograph of Evelyn seated in a ballet studio, wearing a leotard and tights and an old practice tutu, her hands clasping her knees. She is looking down, listening, in that abstracted, thoughtful way she has, to some piece of advice that Henny Jurriens is giving her. He is kneeling in front of her, leaning toward her on one hand, the other hand raised, the thumb and forefinger closed to demonstrate how small, how infinitesimally small, is the refinement he is discussing. His face is animated, concentrated. The photograph catches much of what they meant to each other. She called him her mentor, he called her his genius. They both talked about their relationship in terms of pure love.

On April 9, 1989, Henny Jurriens and his wife Judy were killed in a two-car collision on Highway 75 south of Winnipeg. They were en route to Minneapolis, where Jurriens was to collect the documents declaring him a landed immigrant in Canada. Their three-year-old daughter, Isa, was injured in the accident, but survived.

BRUCE MONK

Henny Jurriens and Evelyn together in the studio.

Evelyn had had a premonition of his death six months previously, in a dream. In the dream, she was riding in a bus with fellow principal dancer Svea Eklof, tour director Mark Porteous, and me. But Henny was missing. So the group of us dismounted from the bus and went in search of him. In the dream, there were trees and a hotel with a fireplace. Upstairs in the hotel, Mark and I broke down a door and found Henny lying dead on the bed.

When he did die, the dream finally made sense. The company members learned about Jurriens's death while they were on tour in Banff, Alberta, deep in the forests of the Rockies. After the news was broken they sat and talked into the small hours beside the big stone fireplace in the hotel where they were staying. Mark Porteous and I escorted Evelyn to Henny's memorial service in Winnipeg.

There were other connections. The quality of the skin on Jurriens's face, in her dream, was exactly how she recalled the feel of her father's cheek when she bent to kiss him at his funeral. And she realized that she had had the dream about Jurriens because she was afraid that, like her father, like anyone else she allowed to become close and important to her, he was going to leave her.

Jurriens had become an integral part of Evelyn's support system, and the abrupt removal of that support was traumatic. "I have to admit," she said later, "I never felt it was possible to feel that much pain. I contemplated not continuing – committing suicide – two or three times. I really wanted to go with him. When you first discover a unique person is gone you feel this incredible void. You think, well I can't survive without that."

But Henny Jurriens will live on always in Evelyn's dancing – in all her dancing, perhaps, but particularly in *The Dying Swan*. Whenever she dances the small and poignant solo that Fokine created for Pavlova, she dances it as a requiem for Henny. She dances Pavlova's dance for Henny, she says, because he and Pavlova approached dance in the same way – as an expression of life in art, as a contribution to human experience. "And in this way," she says, "I know he will never be gone."

Jurriens's death did give her a chance to re-order her priorities and reach a more objective understanding of her situation. Henny, she realized, was all that was really binding her to Winnipeg. He had been her refuge, her support system. His arrival in Winnipeg had coincided with her troubles at the National Ballet of Canada, and he had provided precisely the support she had been unable to find in Toronto. Their partnership had developed into something magical for her, a consistent inspiration. But inspiration had become obligation. She had stayed, perhaps longer than she needed to, because of him. Time, after all, was slipping by. His death released her, and her eventual reaction, once her grief had begun to subside, was relief. With Henny gone, she was able to be more objective about her own goals.

She began to think seriously about redefining her relationship with the company. Initially, her loyalty and her sense that she should try to maintain the directions that Henny had begun took priority. It was difficult for her to think seriously about abandoning Winnipeg. If *she* left, she reasoned, the company's morale, badly shaken by Jurriens's death, would sink even further.

But she also realized that she couldn't be its main support forever, particularly now, when it was inevitably going to undergo radical change. Other people were talking of leaving. There were suggestions that new productions planned by Henny – in particular, a new mounting of *La Bayadère* as a vehicle for Evelyn – would now be cancelled. No one knew who would take over as artistic director.

She also had, for the first time, somewhere to go.

In the summer of 1989 she spent four days with Konstanze Vernon, artistic director of the Bayerische Staatsballett in Munich. They were by no means strangers; they had known each other since the Varna contest in 1980, and it was Vernon who had invited Evelyn to dance *Giselle* in Munich with Richard Cragun at the Heinz Bösl foundation benefit in 1983. But in those four days in 1989 Evelyn felt she had found a new home and a new mentor. It lifted an enormous burden from her shoulders. She realized for the first time how tense she had become over her need to find somewhere to grow.

She knew from experience that she wouldn't be happy with companies in London or Toronto or Amsterdam. But Munich was a different matter. Munich would provide her with a potentially useful footing in Europe. More importantly, she felt that in Munich she had a chance to make progress.

That summer she received an invitation from Peter Schaufuss to appear as a guest with London Festival Ballet (the English National Ballet, as it has since been renamed) in *Swan Lake*. The invitation was another chance to establish herself in London, still one of the centres of the ballet world. But her bad experiences with Sadler's Wells in 1984, and with Schaufuss, the London Festival Ballet, and Makarova in Denmark in 1988, meant she was by no means certain that she wanted to go back.

She knew that if Jurriens had been around he would have urged her to accept the invitation as a challenge, but she wasn't convinced she had the strength to carry it through. The memories were too painful. Maya Plisetskaya, she pointed out, had also had trouble in London – she couldn't finish her thirty-two *fouettés* either, and for that, says Evelyn, she was dismissed, denigrated, made to feel inferior. Plisetskaya refused to go back. Evelyn understood why. She knew her own weaknesses well.

In any case, if she could be as happy and fulfilled in Munich as she had been with Vernon that summer, she didn't need to go to England to prove anything to anyone. If she went to England at all, she would rather go with the RWB or the Munich company, where she could be presented in her own light. And if turning the invitation down meant maybe passing up the only chance of ever going back, she didn't care.

So no, she said; thank you, but no.

Two months after the death of Jurriens and his wife, David Peregrine was killed in an accident in his own light aircraft in Alaska. With Peregrine at the controls and his brother Meirig and a young dancer from the Louisville Ballet as passengers, the aircraft flew into a mountainside. No one survived.

Evelyn subsequently said she had "made her peace" with David Peregrine before he died. However, Peregrine had remained deeply wounded by the break-up of their performing partnership and there was widespread regret, among friends of them both, that there would always be something between them that would remain unfinished.

Although their friendship was long ended, Peregrine's death, coming so soon after the death of Jurriens, reinforced Evelyn's own sense of mortality, never far from the surface. She put a brave face on it all, but the sense of personal loss was acute, and she continued to have moments of great doubt.

One day in Munich that summer, she had a dream in which Jurriens came backstage, took her aside into a dressing room, and said, "They told me up there that you have been a real crusader since I've been away, but don't worry, I'm back now and everything's okay." She knew, even in the dream, that this wasn't true, however much she might have wished it, and she woke weeping. Later the same day, at ballet class, news arrived of a gold medal success at Varna for one of the young Munich dancers. Vulnerable, depressed, and feeling terribly alone, Evelyn collapsed in tears. All she could think of was David and Henny and her own inevitable aging. She was inconsolable.

She continued to have fears about moving away from Winnipeg. She had stayed so long because there was nowhere else she could be certain of support, and she was still scared Europe might simply swallow her up. But Vernon and the Munich company gave her the sense that she had found someone who, like Henny, was willing to help her grow. Munich also offered a new atmosphere, a company without the accumulated emotional baggage of all those Winnipeg years.

Vernon herself was urging the move. She made Evelyn see she had been spending too much energy on trying to hold the RWB together. "You are not ready to be a mother yet," Vernon told her. "You have ten years left to do what you must do for the world and for your art." Evelyn realized then, she says, that "that's what Henny was trying to tell me in the dream: just dance, just do your job."

Close advisers warned her it was probably not wise to cut herself loose from the support system she had established in Winnipeg. But with Henny gone, she asked, how much of a support system was left? Mark Porteous was a wonderful and devoted friend, but he was unable to help her with her professional decisions. There was a possibility that company regisseur Alla Savchenko (one of the triumvirate of artistic staff that stepped in to run the company when Jurriens died) might develop into that kind of adviser, but that wasn't something Evelyn could count on.

Late in 1989 she decided to throw in her lot with the Munich company. After fourteen years with the RWB, her sense of responsibility was finally gone, and with it had gone her competitive feelings toward the National Ballet. She had done what she could for as long as she was able. Her renewed connection with Vernon had given her new hope. She felt she was being offered a second chance, and she didn't want to jeopardize it. She was ready for the next step up.

In the bad times, Evelyn often seemed to survive on sheer mental muscle (though her mother always used to worry that the physical effects of anorexia

DAVID COOPER

Evelyn with her RWB colleague Mark Godden in Piano Variations III, *by Hans van Manen.*

might affect her mental capacities too). Her colleagues talk of seeing her dine on a bag of cookies. And while there is every likelihood of her being able to dance well into her forties, as long as her body remains healthy, many had worried that anorexia could be a stumbling-block in her progress. "I wish someone could get it into her head that there's a certain point where she begins to look ugly," Toronto critic Michael Crabb once commented. He mentioned seeing her doing *Elite Syncopations* with the Sadler's Wells company in London. "She had put on maybe three or four pounds, and it gave her just enough shape – she looked extraordinarily sexy."

But now, technically, emotionally, and physically, she was ready as well. She had been working on her physical placement, straightening her pelvis. Her weight was unchanged, but the change in her bodily alignment gave her a fuller, healthier look. And the rawness of her response on the stage, the rawness that many had seen as an essential element of her artistry, had been replaced by a more practised ease.

It is possible that this ease came from a new self-respect that psychotherapy had helped her find. She found her fears had diminished and discovered a new enjoyment in what she did. At the same time, she had more control over her emotions, and more control over her technical abilities. Where she once had to rely on instinct to serve her, now she was able to make a mood consciously, from a position of control. The loss of the exposed raw nerve that had been such a part of her appeal on the stage no longer mattered; she had passed through that phase. Without losing any of the communicativeness, she had gained the confidence, and the ability, to summon at will what once was far beyond her control.

Eight months after Jurriens's death she was finally able to make the break. On tour with the RWB in Fredericton, New Brunswick, she told the interim artistic director, André Lewis, of her decision to devote half her time in the 1990-91 season to Munich, and half to Winnipeg.

The week she made her decision, she had another dream about Henny. She was at his memorial service with her mother, cradling her mother's head on her shoulder, comforting her like a child. At some point in the service, Evelyn felt it necessary to leave in search of someone, she didn't know who. The journey took her through doors, through catacombs on her hands and knees, through small spaces. And when she turned round to come back, she found the spaces she had passed through had become too small to allow her to return. The people she had relied on were no longer within reach. She was in a new place – alone.

*Half-hidden behind her art, in performance as in life, Evelyn shimmers into infinity
in this David Cooper study.*

CODA

Oleg Vinogradov, the artistic director and chief choreographer of Leningrad's Kirov Ballet, maintains a spacious country *dacha* in a tiny village about an hour's drive from Leningrad. Its hallway and staircases are lined with poster-size pictures of his favourite dancers. Most of them are of women from his company, but in the prize position at the top of the stairs is a picture of Evelyn Hart, in a pose from *Swan Lake*.

In June 1990, Evelyn finally made her debut on the Kirov Theatre stage, at the head of the company that nurtured her, with Rex Harrington as her guest partner. As part of the RWB's tour of Eastern Europe and the U.S.S.R., they danced Rudi van Dantzig's *Romeo and Juliet*, first at Moscow's Stanislavsky Theatre, then at the Kirov Theatre in Leningrad.

The Moscow engagement marked the first time the RWB had performed in Russia since 1968, and members of the company talked of butterflies and goosebumps at the challenge of bringing classical ballet to its motherland. John Meehan, who had succeeded Henny Jurriens as artistic director early in 1990, said the Moscow opening was "the first time I have felt nervous for this company. I know how well we do *Romeo* – but we are also doing it in Moscow."

By contrast, Evelyn seemed surprisingly nonchalant. Luxuriating in the prospect of dancing the ideal role with the ideal partner in the ideal setting, she was happy and relaxed.

Harrington, with much riding on the Soviet performances, confessed to being both excited and nervous. But his nerves were not apparent on opening night. All ardent youth and unmannered nobility, he seemed to release Evelyn into some transcendental otherworld where she was free to create images giving visible form to innocence, trust, and love. For Evelyn, the Moscow opening performance was "the best I have ever done. Dancing with Rex is a dream."

The audience adored them. In typical Russian style, they set up a sustained rhythmic clapping, deluged Evelyn with flowers, demanded curtain-call after curtain-call, then melted away gradually until only a small group of enthusiasts remained at the front of the stalls. Backstage, a large crowd of wellwishers waited to shower Hart with more flowers and compliments and to seek autographs.

Russian ballet legend Asaf Messerer, now a teacher at the Bolshoi Ballet, watched the show from the front row and praised the company's polished style and the clarity and theatricality of van Dantzig's production. "Audiences here are very discriminating," said the Canadian ambassador, Vernon G. Turner, "but this company has won them over. It is a great piece of ambassadorship for Canada – a major Canadian company giving a brilliant performance of a major work of art."

A week later they performed in Leningrad. The Kirov Theatre is the launching-pad of much of ballet as we know it in the modern world. It was the home of Serge Diaghilev and many of the dancers, composers, and designers he lured to the West as part of his Ballets Russes. And it is a living shrine to the Vaganova legacy, the nurturing-ground of Nureyev, Makarova, and Baryshnikov and, in an earlier era, of Nijinsky and Anna Pavlova. For Evelyn even more than for the RWB, this was a historic moment, and she did not fail.

The Leningrad audience, accustomed to excellence, received the first two acts coolly but politely. But at the end of the evening the audience in the elegant gold-and-blue auditorium erupted into an eight-minute standing ovation for Hart.

"Little Miss Leningrad" had reached her spiritual home.

In Munich, on the other hand, the blessings were mixed.

Artistically, all seemed well. She was able to dance in four full-length classical ballets in quick succession, an opportunity she would never get in Winnipeg. She danced the lead role in the world première of a Munich production of *Cinderella* and was delighted to have Harrington as her guest partner for the performance. She won the Munich critics' Star of the Week award for her portrayal of Tatiana in *Onegin*, and the Rose of the Week award for her performance of the White Swan pas de deux at a Tchaikovsky gala in Munich.

But despite these accolades she was far from happy. Thousands of miles from home, she was lonely. She found it hard to make friends. Her off-beat sense of humour didn't go down well with her new colleagues – "Germans are very nice people," she said later, "but they're not crazy. I would tell someone a joke and they would just gaze at me like I was nuts."

At the simplest level was a problem of language. Evelyn initially intended to learn German – Konstanze Vernon gave her a set of German-language tapes as a gift after the *Cinderella* première – but despite the best of intentions she never managed to find time to sit down and study. Work was always in the way.

She discovered, however, that the obsessive devotion that has caused her estrangement from so many partners had no place in Munich. The system was simply not equipped to deal with people who wanted to work that intensely. Both dancers and artistic staff considered her odd. Often, at the theatre, there simply wasn't enough to do. In her last four performing weeks in 1990, she danced only six performances – a standard amount in many large ballet companies, where leading roles must be shared among a large number of principal dancers, but nowhere near enough to satisfy Evelyn.

She began to modify her tiny company apartment near the theatre to make it look more like her apartment in Winnipeg – a similar colour scheme, virtually identical furniture. It became important to surround herself with things that made her feel comfortable, that made the apartment feel like home. When a man from the company called to collect her to take her to the airport, she saw how taken-aback he was at her decorating choices – the draped red satin, the black lacquer, a style she calls "old theatre, or maybe western brothel." "I could see he was . . . well, the Bavarians have a distinct style," she says, "and it's certainly not western brothel."

Her lack of confidence meant that she saw every young Munich star-to-be as a challenge. Most of the dancers who alternated with her in the lead roles of the classics were in their teens, "and all of a sudden I was so aware of how old I was." It didn't matter that Konstanze Vernon had warned her from the start that she wanted Evelyn in the company as an example for her youngsters to aspire to. The fact of it simply accentuated her loneliness. "It's as if they're looking at you as something they can buy," she told me, "and they use it for their purposes, but they don't feel responsibility for what's going on inside you. It's the whole mentality of putting people in boxes. I think that's why Winnipeg has been so important. The people around me have not put me in a box, and I understand now how lucky I have been to be in that atmosphere."

By the time she returned to Winnipeg that Christmas, midway through her first season as resident guest artist in Munich, she was giving serious consideration to staying home.

She had gone to Munich with the hope that she could make it the jumping-off point for a new phase of her career in the ballet-houses of Europe, but she had quickly come to realize this would be more difficult than she had first thought – there were fewer guesting and gala opportunities than in North America, and far more ballerinas competing for them.

In any case, she was by no means sure that she wanted the pressure of that kind of career. Her approach had become fatalistic. If it was meant to be, it would happen. Meanwhile, the RWB still provided her with the chance to learn, to grow, to accomplish new things.

She struggled with these thoughts throughout the Christmas and New Year season of Winnipeg performances, performances in which she displayed a burnished maturity and brilliance of style in Galina Yordanova's new mounting of the Kingdom of the Shades act from *La Bayadère*, and, partnered by Mark Godden, invested *Valse Triste*, a piece of gala choreography by Peter Martins, with an unexpectedly moving resonance.

Valse Triste is a trifle in which a pensive girl in a black dress is visited by a white-clad figure, perhaps an imagined lover, perhaps the spirit of someone gone. In Evelyn's mind it was the figure of Henny Jurriens – and it was in the spirit of Henny Jurriens that she finally composed herself as her Winnipeg visit drew to an end.

The visit had been a time for pause and reflection, a time to realize that the Munich experience would probably prove to be, despite its challenges, one of the most important moves of her career. It was easy to become disheartened, to feel disadvantaged. But as Henny had always told her, there would be problems wherever she went. The important thing was not to brood on them, but to learn how to cope, to develop the strength to take the risks and not give up on them too early.

By the time the date of her return to Munich arrived, she had reached a new point of confidence. "It's like wearing the ruby slippers," she said, "and finally waking up and realizing you had the power from the very beginning, but you had to go through incredible voyages and trials and fears and frights and illnesses to discover that power." She boarded the aircraft that would carry her back to Germany with a lightened heart.

This is not by any means the end of the story. It is only the end of a stage in Evelyn's difficult and brilliant career. Despite the odds against her, the fears within her, and the external obstacles she has faced, she has accomplished what she set out to do – to dance superbly, to bring a rare emotional expressiveness to Canadian ballet, and to dance on the world's major stages. Thus far it has been a story of the values and sacrifices inherent in a life in art. It is both an inspirational and a cautionary tale for those who dream, as Evelyn once did, of becoming a prima ballerina. We leave her now, poised for new challenges, new ways of accepting and celebrating her artistry, new ways of reaching serenity.

But happy ever after, the way it is in fairy tales, the way it is in dreams? Only the future will show.

INDEX

Page numbers of photographs are in bold face.